HIDDEN DANGERS

HIDDEN DANGERS

COMBATING THREATS TO HEALTHY RELATIONSHIPS

KIM BECKHAM

LEAFWOOD PUBLISHERS
an imprint of Abilene Christian University Press

HIDDEN DANGERS

Combating Threats to Healthy Relationships

LEAFWOOD PUBLISHERS
an imprint of Abilene Christian University Press

ISBN 978-0-89112-349-1 | LCCN 2015012615

Printed in the United States of America

Published in association with WordWise Media Services, 4083 Avenue L, Suite 255, Lancaster, CA 93536.

LIBRARY OF CONGRESS CATALOGING-IN-PUBLICATION DATA
Beckham, Kim, 1953-
Hidden dangers : combating threats to healthy relationships / Kim Beckham.
pages cm
Includes bibliographical references and index.
ISBN 978-0-89112-349-1 (alk. paper)
1. Interpersonal relations--Religious aspects--Christianity. 2. Emotions--Religious aspects--Christianity. I. Title.
BV4597.52.B434 2015
158.2--dc23

2015012615

Cover design by Thinkpen Design, LLC
Interior text design by Sandy Armstrong, Strong Design

Leafwood Publishers is an imprint of Abilene Christian University Press
ACU Box 29138, Abilene, Texas 79699

1-877-816-4455 | www.leafwoodpublishers.com

25 26 27 28 29 30 / 7 6 5 4 3 2

Table of Contents

INTRODUCTION

When I was eight years old, our family lived in the country. My brothers and I loved getting to run free on the acres of forest and undeveloped meadows around our home. One of our favorite spots was a tiny creek that ran through a small ravine about half a mile from our house. Someone had rigged a rope that you could swing across the ravine and land with an impressive leap across the shallow water. Then you could rush back across the creek and up a five-foot-high embankment to reach the rope and swing again.

One day, as we were enjoying the excitement of the rope across the creek, I had an experience that would stay with me all of my life. While running back across the creek after swinging, I started up the side of the slope and pulled myself up to the last step on the climb. As I stepped to the top, my eyes fell on a pile of large sticks lying on the flat area just inches from my face. My eye caught a slight movement and, to my horror, I was face-to-face with a large, black snake. It was one of the cottonmouth water moccasins that populate the East Texas woods, and I knew the danger was real.

The water moccasin is one of the three venomous snakes native to East Texas, and its bite is painful and potentially fatal. I was less than one foot from its ugly head, and if he chose to strike, there wouldn't be time to move out of his way. Then I realized that we had been running right by the snake for the last several minutes and hadn't even seen it as we charged up the slope. I held my breath and waited to see what that fat, black snake would do. Fortunately, it turned and slithered off the embankment in the opposite direction from my panicked face. It took thirty minutes to calm down and go back to swinging with my brothers. But when I did, I watched for snakes with much greater caution than I had before.

I've never forgotten that experience and one of the lessons I took from that day. It is possible to have very dangerous things hidden just inches from you. That is what this book is about—exposing the relationship-killers to which we are often oblivious.

We live in a time of relationship meltdowns. Most of us have relationship struggles with friends or family. Outsiders can often easily see the causes of the painful struggles endured by others. Yet those in the midst of strife may not even notice the problems. The truth is that having deep and satisfying connections with the significant people in our lives is complicated.

Everyone knows the relationship deal breakers—infidelity and betrayal. Few of us are surprised when relationships are damaged by cruelty or gossip. But many of us find ourselves perplexed by the relationships that fall apart when there seems to be no apparent reason. There are many ways to weaken or damage those delicate ties. In over thirty years of counseling and leading people in all kinds of relationships, I have witnessed the hidden dangers in healthy relationships that often go unnoticed until it's too late. I am writing this book to bring some of these relational land mines to the surface.

It is my hope that as you read about the hidden dangers revealed in the pages that follow, you will find ways to strengthen the connections of your life. Each chapter includes helpful exercises to cement new insights into your mind and to put them into practice with loved ones. Let's get started exposing those hidden dangers that can ruin your most treasured relationships.

"You must love yourself before you love another. By accepting yourself and fully being what you are, your simple presence can make others happy."

—Anonymous

Chapter One

THE INFERIORITY COMPLEX

How can you love someone else when you don't like yourself?

An inferiority complex can be thought of as poor self-esteem. Positive self-esteem—thinking of ourselves and valuing ourselves highly—is crucial in relationships because it gives us the ability to fight when we face overwhelming odds. Sometimes it seems there is nothing we can do to resolve a struggle in our marriage, to help our children get in line, or to resolve conflict among friends. High self-esteem is a powerful weapon to help us face all these problems. With it, no situation can keep us from seeing ourselves as strong, capable, and deserving. High self-esteem allows us to feel comfortable with high levels of success. It confirms our desire to fulfill our capabilities, and it won't let us rest if we have done the wrong thing.

Former First Lady Eleanor Roosevelt spoke wisely when she said, "No one can make you feel inferior without your consent." Still, so many of us feel inferior. We feel that we're not good-looking enough, or smart enough, or even spiritual enough for people to love us. In reality, the trouble is we don't love ourselves. And if we don't love ourselves, our ability to love others is hindered. As a result, our relationships are put in jeopardy.

- How is your self-esteem?
- Is your insecurity in relationships a result of poor self-esteem?

The primary driver of strong marital relationships is intimacy. We all yearn to get close and build lasting connections. The Bible says, "Nevertheless neither is the man without the woman, neither the woman without the man, in the Lord" (1 Cor. 11:11 KJV). This is a clear teaching that we are meant to be connected. Yet sometimes an inferiority complex—in one partner or both—can sabotage intimacy.

What does an inferiority complex in a marriage look like? It may take many forms: "I can't trust you because I'm not attractive enough to hold your attention." "I can't tell the truth; I have to rely on lies instead of on love to keep our relationship going." "I have to find ways to destroy this healthy relationship because I'm not worthy of being loved." It could even be: "I must stay in this destructive relationship even to the point of physical danger because I'm not good enough for anyone else. No one will want me if I leave my abusive spouse."

Sometimes we're afraid to show our flaws. To avoid revealing them, we do all we can to mask our weaknesses. This behavior can also sabotage our potential to be close to and achieve true intimacy with others. We need to love ourselves enough, and trust others enough, to let our true selves show—faults included.

Parents can even have inferiority issues. We are living in the Age of the Child. In my generation, the rule for children was, "Be quiet." "Stay out of the way." "Don't cause any commotion." "If we want to talk with you, we'll speak with you first." Today, it's a different story. Kids rule the roost! Mom and Dad can't seem to live their lives without checking first with their children. It's good to do all we can for our children, but not if our sole purpose is to be perfect parents with perfect children.

Many parents don't enjoy their children for the unique people that they are. They use and want their children to serve as ego boosters. These types of parents do not love their children as individuals but only as a reflection of great parenting. Behind closed doors, some parents may sound like this: "You're not pretty enough." "You're not as good as your sister." "You're not smart." "You're no athlete." Many children feel as if nothing they do pleases their parents. If they get a B on their report card, it should have been an A. If they get an A, it should have been an A plus. If they score a touchdown playing football, they should have scored two. If this continues, the child may develop feelings of "I'm not worth anything."

This negative talk creates a hole in our children's hearts—a hole that grows larger as they become adults. As adults, many of us are like donuts. We may look okay on the outside because we're glazed over, but inside is a huge hole and feelings of unworthiness. Where did these feelings come from? They started with our parents. Disapproving, negative remarks and evaluations of behavior that emphasize mistakes and shortcomings can seriously damage children's self-esteem even before they reach the age of six!

As adults, if we ever want to get past the pain that is currently undermining our relationships, we need to look at our parents first as humans. Look back and say, "My parents did the best they could, but they weren't perfect. They didn't know everything. They made mistakes, but I don't have to live my life based on mistakes they made by overemphasizing my mistakes and shortcomings."

Another area of struggle is feeling inferior about our own self-image. All of us look different. Few of us look like movie stars. Some of us have real physical needs, such as an inability to walk or a speech impediment. All of these can cause deep feelings of inferiority.

When I was a kid, I wasn't handsome. I grew up really fast—and I mean *up*! At fourteen, I was six feet, three inches tall and weighed 127 pounds. I was a real string bean. On top of that, I had terrible acne—talk about an inferiority complex! But through it all, I learned how to smile and let my personality shine through. I discovered there were people smart enough to see me with their hearts, which is an important lesson. We need to remember that *everyone* sees us differently, due to their own experiences and preferences. What we think is a personal defect may not be a defect at all when viewed through the heart of another.

The same holds true for our intellectual capacity. So much harm is done in the classroom when students feel ranked or judged by the academic achievements of others. Our teachers do great work, but they can't do it all. So much of our educational system is based on mental acuity. We need to set other measures of success—such as the ability to be compassionate and the ability to build good relationships.

- Do you see others with your eyes or your heart?
- Do you use your personality to connect with others?
- Do you know someone who uses looks or material things to connect with others?

Have you ever sat through a "hellfire and damnation" sermon? It's the kind of sermon that focuses solely on our sinfulness. Perhaps the most serious cause of an inferiority complex is the feeling that God can't love us because we are not worthy. That's a poor understanding of Scripture, but some people truly feel they deserve God's wrath and punishment. If you feel that way, you're not alone. Even biblical people felt they were unworthy—and inferior.

In the Old Testament, Moses stood before the burning bush, which, if you remember, symbolized the presence of God. God said to Moses, "I want you to lead the Israelites out of bondage. I'm going to empower you." Moses had many excuses for why he couldn't go. He said, "I'm a stutterer." God said, in essence, "Well, listen—if you're worried about stuttering, I made your mouth and I can fix it. But if that's a problem, we'll send Aaron with you, and he can do the talking." But in fact, Aaron did not end up doing all of the talking. The first time Moses and Aaron met with the nation of Israel, Aaron did the talking, and in their early encounters with Pharaoh they are both present and perhaps he spoke for Moses. But it appears that God restored Moses's self-esteem. As the conflict continued, Moses is shown speaking directly to Pharaoh again and again. It appears that Moses did not need Aaron as a crutch any longer. God removed Moses's feeling of inferiority as he obediently followed him. How many of us *truly* believe God can take away our inferiority complexes?

God created us and stamped us with *his* image. There is no other living creature comparable in the entire universe; not even the angels compare to us in complexity and glory. We have been chosen—and God further affirmed our chosen-ness by sending his Son, Jesus Christ, to live among us and die for us. "But you are a chosen generation, a royal priesthood, a holy nation, His own special people, that you may proclaim the praises of Him who called you out of darkness into His marvelous light" (1 Pet. 2:9). Our self-esteem increases when we understand that God has chosen us. He created us in his image. He sent his only Son to us. If God loves us that much, how can we have poor self-esteem?

Remember the movie *Pay It Forward* released by Warner Brothers in 2000? It tells a moving story of a young man who tries to help others and how each good deed he does leads someone else to do something kind for others in return. It reminds us that there is really nothing we can do to pay back what we owe God and others. So we pay it forward. When we do something to serve others, it creates good feelings within and counteracts feelings of inferiority. If we don't like who we are, one of the best ways to change that feeling is to serve other people. That means helping those in need of help, whoever they may be. When we unselfishly serve others, we pay it forward and increase our self-esteem.

The power of prayer can also help us pay it forward. One thing I've learned about prayer is that it's about asking God and giving God room to answer: "Ask and you shall receive." It is also about reconnecting to the place where we feel truly loved by God. And when we enter into that place, we enable God to deepen our self-esteem.

The more we enter into the house of God (a house whose language is prayer), the less dependent we are on the blame or praise of those who surround us. We are also more free to let our whole being be filled with that first love—the love of Christ. As long as we wonder what other people say or think about us, or try to act in ways that elicit a positive response, we are allowing others to control our self-esteem. And in that dark world, our surroundings dictate our self-worth. Those who do not have a strong self-worth and self-esteem cling to the false hope that more success, more praise, and more satisfaction will result in the love they crave. This thinking breeds greed, bitterness, and, often, violence.

However, prayer will reveal again and again that the love we are looking for has already been given to us and that we can come to God to experience that love. Prayer is entering into communion with the one who molded each being in the womb with love and only love. In the presence of God, we experience real love and discover what God sees in us. We are not created out of our experiences and out of the rejections and acceptances of those around us. Instead, we are rooted in the one who called us into being.

Exercise

Practice serving others. See the openings and pay it forward. Maybe it's listening to a friend with a heavy heart. Maybe it's giving of yourself in the community. You can volunteer to feed the hungry at a soup kitchen. You could even help house the homeless through Habitat for Humanity or love the loveless with a visit to the local jail. Take the steps to serve. Then write down how serving makes you feel about yourself. For more, see 1 Corinthians 2:1–4, Exodus 19:5, Revelation 1:6, and Acts 20:28.

"I never knew how to worship until I knew how to love."
—Henry Ward Beecher

Chapter Two

SELFISHNESS

It's hard to build a relationship for two when all you think about is you.

We are all vulnerable to selfishness. It's an age-old trait that is evident everywhere. In Luke 15, the Lord recounts a classic tale of a father's love for his errant, sin-filled son. Yet on closer examination, the story also is a perfect illustration of selfishness.

> A man had two sons; the younger said to his father, "Father, give me my inheritance." So he gave it to him. The son then journeyed to a far country and wasted his possessions with wild living. . . . There arose a famine in that land and he began to be in want. The son was reduced to feeding swine and even trying to steal their food out of his desperate hunger. When he came to himself he said, how many of my father's

> hired servants have bread enough to spare, and I am starving. I will go to my father and say, "Father, I have sinned against heaven and before you. I am no longer worthy to be called your son. Make me like one of your hired servants."
>
> He came to his father's house, but while still a great way off, his father saw him and ran out and kissed him. The son said, "Father, I have sinned against heaven and am no longer worthy to be called your son." But the father said, "Bring out the best robe and put it on him and put a ring on his hand and sandals on his feet and bring a young calf and kill it for a feast. For my son was dead and is alive again. He was lost but now is found." And they rejoiced. (Luke 15:11–24, my paraphrase)

While we see the great heart of God in this passage, we can also feel the gross selfishness of a son who prematurely demanded his inheritance and lived without concern for his father or others. A son who foolishly wasted everything on sinful and selfish living.

More evidence of selfishness can be found in the reaction of the older brother in the story. In verses 28–30, it says,

> But he [the older brother] was angry and would not go in. Therefore his father came out and pleaded with him. So he answered and said to his father, "Lo, these many years I have been serving you; I never transgressed your commandment at any time; and

> yet you never gave me a young goat, that I might make merry with my friends. But as soon as this son of yours came, who has devoured your livelihood with harlots, you killed the fatted calf for him."

Just as the father in this wonderful biblical story welcomes his son after wasteful living, our Savior welcomes us back with open arms in spite of all we do that is selfish. Our selfish behavior prevents us from having healthy marriages and friendships and can prevent us from being effective parents. If left unchecked, selfishness will poison otherwise healthy relationships.

- What was the last selfish request you made in a relationship?
- How are your relationships? Are you the first to forgive, or do you hold out to get your way?

Through the years, I have watched my wife garden. She is a talented gardener and can work with all types of plants. I have learned from watching her work that certain vines are so voracious that they overtake the flower bed and choke every living thing in the garden. Selfishness is like such a vine. It grows in our lives, sometimes without recognition, and it can destroy every decent and good thing. It is a hidden danger in our relationships.

While the vines that choke a plant may be clearly evident, selfishness of the spirit is usually harder to spot. One way self-ishness becomes evident is when we try to live with others. In a community, like a church, we are forced to be around many people. Someone else is always there. We cannnot be constantly thinking, *What do I want? What do I need? Why don't they always do it the way I like?* We have to learn to live with others and do what is best for the group, not just for the individual. The best way for us to spot selfishness is to refuse to live in isolation. Then we will encounter the need for giving and a demand for compromise. Living with a community or group forces us to deal with and address our selfishness.

The same is true in a marriage. For a marriage to be successful, we have to come to grips with selfishness. The other person is always there, there, there. Two different people are living together 24/7, two people who have to organize a life together. This is the smallest community of all. When we live with other people and try to build relationships, they *will* test our selfishness.

In a marriage, one partner cannot always have his or her own way. Because each of us is raised in a unique family culture, we all come to our marriages with deeply set preferences as to food choices or how we celebrate holidays. Perhaps our selfishness will be tested when our lifelong habit of having fish on Friday night finds itself confronted by our mate's preference for steak on the weekends. Or our selfishness will be challenged when we find that our family tradition of opening presents on Christmas Eve comes into conflict with our mate's beloved habit of opening presents on Christmas morning. In hundreds of ways, both big and small, marriage will test our selfishness. If we don't learn to compromise and see the other person's point of view, we can find our union in real conflict.

In his incredible book *Blue Like Jazz*, Donald Miller wrote of his insight into selfishness.

> Living in community made me realize one of my faults. I was addicted to myself. All I thought about was myself. The only thing I really cared about was myself. I had very little concept of love, altruism, or sacrifice. I discovered that my mind is like a radio that picks up only one station, the one that plays me, Donald Miller, K-DON all the time.[1]

We are like that. K-ME, me all the time. We play one kind of music: self, all the time.

If you are selfish, you have trouble or difficulty paying attention when people you care about are expressing their feelings. It bores you to listen to their difficulties. You may constantly check your watch during church or during conversations with others. You impatiently wait for the person who is talking to stop so you can get a word in. And it's been a long time since you went out of your way to help someone who couldn't give you something in return.

You seldom volunteer to help friends, church, or charities with projects because your time is so important. You rarely consider how things affect others. Loved ones rarely please you because they seldom meet your expectations. Your love and affection for your spouse is conditioned on how he or she pleases you and meets your needs. The success of your children (you think) is gauged by how they reflect on you. Anyone who gives you a gift must want something in return, and giving gifts to people in your circle is wasteful. You use people and love things instead of the other way around. You refuse to extend yourself to protect the weak when others at work or school pick on them. Every conversation is turned toward you or your concerns.

Selfishness. It's rampant. It's not new. Throughout history and the Bible, there are many examples of selfishness. For example, Adam and Eve committed the first act of selfishness against humankind. In Genesis 3:5–6, it says,

> "For God knows that in the day you eat of it your eyes will be opened, and you will be like God, knowing good and evil." So when the woman saw that the tree was good for food, that it was pleasant to the eyes, and a tree desirable to make one wise, she took of its fruit and ate. She also gave to her husband with her, and he ate.

When Adam and Eve considered what was in it for them, they ate. *It looks good and it will make me wise. I'll forget what God has said. I'll just do it my way.* And so, they plunged the world into sin. Theirs was the ultimate selfishness.

Looking closely at our sinful intentions, we realize they are selfish at the core. When we sin—just like Adam and Eve—we are putting ourselves before God, our community, and really anyone else. In the garden, Adam and Eve did exactly what they wanted to do, making themselves the highest priority. "Looking out for number one" can become a disease of the soul if we make ourselves the center of the universe. The essential spiritual battle is always that of moving away from self-absorption toward God and the needs of others. If we reflect, we can probably recognize selfish behavior. And when we are able to admit our selfishness, how do we then combat it?

There are three simple rules. First, fall in love with Jesus Christ. When you fall in love with Christ, he can break the power of selfishness. God makes us new creatures in Christ. He is love incarnate, which is the opposite of selfishness. The story of Zacchaeus, a crooked tax collector, in Luke 19 shows how God *can* change us. Zacchaeus was stealing from others, but when Jesus appeared to him, he was changed and offered to give back fourfold the amount he had stolen. He was so transformed that he said, "I'll give away whatever I have." The cycle of selfishness was broken when Zacchaeus fell in love with Christ.

When we fall in love with Christ and what he wants for us, rather than with what we want for ourselves, it enables us to live the kind of life that God desires of us. Going forward from our conversion, we can carefully choose the actions that lead us closer to Christ—closer to living a selfless life. In Jesus' own words, "Whoever loses their life for my sake will find it" (Matt. 10:39 NIV). The great philosopher Alexander Smellie said, "If I really love God, my innate and persistent selfishness will have received its death-blow."

It is impossible to *truly* love Christ and remain selfish. His words and deeds form a picture of the epitome of unselfishness. He prompts his followers to give, to serve, and to care about others. There are many references in the Bible about love growing and flowing from those in his service. When you fall in love with Jesus Christ—not just memorizing a creed or joining a church, but *really* falling in love with the living Savior and walking with him each day—selfishness will disappear because the heart of God will dwell within your soul.

The second rule for transforming a selfish heart: fall in love with helping others. If we fall in love with doing nice things for others, we will also get rid of our innate selfishness. When you begin the practice of helping with the needs of others in your daily life, you will experience great levels of contentment and self-satisfaction. Look around and notice those people who are truly happy. They are most likely involved in a cause greater than themselves. People who spend time serving with others who are service-oriented build a network of generous, caring people that can make a difference.

Find a way to help someone else today. Volunteer; sign up for a job that no one else wants to do. If you are married, go home and serve your spouse. Look around in your community and find a way to serve. Most of us in the U.S. are beyond blessed. There are so many opportunities to give of our time, our talents, and our income. Fall in love with the act of giving of yourself.

When was the last time you helped others and it made you feel good? Maybe you donated a gift to the victims of the earthquake in Haiti. Perhaps you gave to your church or some fine charity like Habitat for Humanity. A church, a community, your colleagues, your friends, your spouse, or even a stranger—all provide many opportunities to give by helping others. Next time you find yourself stuck in traffic, let another car move in front of yours. Perhaps next time you go through the drive-through of a fast food restaurant, when you reach the window, offer to pay for the next person in line. Find joy in doing simple things for others.

A third way to combat selfishness is to fall in love with service. There are many biblical examples of service. John the Baptist was willing to serve Jesus when he gave up his crowd of followers so that Jesus might have a larger following. The apostle Andrew's quiet service was responsible for bringing his renowned brother, Peter, to Christ. We rarely hear of Andrew again in the Bible, perhaps because he was so busy serving others.

- When was the last time you gave and it made you feel good?
- When was the last time you performed a random act of kindness? How did it make you feel?

One of the most effective ways of combating selfishness is to perform anonymous acts of service. Visit a retirement center and go room to room offering a rose to every resident. Prepare a meal and take it to your local fire station. Tell them it is from the entire neighborhood and that you appreciate their service. Just make sure no one in your circle of friends knows of your acts of service. Let it be a secret between you and God, and your selfishness will diminish.

Service can be many things. It can be deliberately taking the worst parking space in the shopping center so that others may have the best. It can be picking up litter and trash in the parking lot at your place of business. It can be sending an anonymous financial gift to a college student in need. It can be volunteering at a local nonprofit. You can even offer to babysit the children of a young single mother for free.

All of these selfless acts will help you fall in love with service. And when we fall in love with Christ, with helping others, and with the act of service, selfishness will no longer dictate our actions. Service will become second nature. Service will help rid us of the greedy thorns of selfishness in our souls.

Exercise

Think of three unselfish acts you can perform within the next week. When each one is completed, write how it makes you feel. For more, see Romans 13:12–14, Amos 6:4–6, and Colossians 3:5.

"How much more grievous are the consequences of anger than the causes of it."
—Marcus Aurelius

Note

[1]Donald Miller, *Blue Like Jazz* (Nashville: Thomas Nelson, 2003), 181.

Chapter Three

ANGER IN OUR RELATIONSHIPS

"He that hath no rule over his own spirit is like a city that is broken down, and without walls."
—Proverbs 25:28 KJV

Years ago, while living in Aubrey, Texas, I pulled into a station to fill my car with gas. I noticed a man with his car jacked up, trying to change his tire. He had just a simple little lug wrench, and it kept slipping off. I watched him from across the way and could even hear him talking to the tire. All of a sudden, the tire slipped off and the man skinned his hand. He jumped up, took the lug wrench, and began to physically attack his car. He smashed the rearview mirror off the car and shattered the windshield. Then he kicked the car off the jack, while screaming and cursing at it. I wanted to laugh, but I was afraid he would hear me. I thought, wow, that guy has lost it! It was a classic display of the destructive power of anger.

We live in a world of relationships: culture to culture, family to family, friend to friend, colleague to colleague, and beloved to beloved. Yet for many of us, our relationships are as fragile as glass. We spend too much of our time breaking them and making more damage, then trying to pick up the pieces.

Gregory the Great, a sixth-century Christian scholar, gave us some insight into relationship destruction with his compilation of the seven deadly sins: pride, envy, anger, sloth, greed, gluttony, and lust. Of all of the sins that can poison our relationships, perhaps the greatest toxin is anger. Often, those who succumb to anger don't even *know* that they are angry.

Anger is an interesting subject in our culture because for most of us, it is an acceptable weakness. In fact, people brag about having a short fuse or an "Irish temper." Sometimes they'll say, "Oh, you have to understand, I 'go off.'" It's almost as if they're proud of their anger.

- When was the last time you really lost your temper? What did you feel?
- Did you damage something or someone? Do you regret your actions?
- Could you express your sorrow and repair the physical damage or the relationship?

The last time I lost my temper was during an argument with a staff member. My adrenal glands were pumping about a gallon a second, and I felt engulfed in flames. Anger is like that. It's hot and it's toxic. For those who inadvertently stand too close to us when we erupt, anger can burn and scar. After my eruption came feelings of guilt. I realized that regardless of the issues we had discussed and the bad behavior of my employee, I had failed to control my emotions and anger had gotten the best of me.

In his book *The Sins We Love*, Randy Rowland wrote about anger. He said, "I hate who I am when I express anger inappropriately. I cannot conceive how to discuss it with those I've hurt or revisit the circumstances for self-improvement. The flame of anger flashes outward, but the same flame licks away at the heart, soul, and mind of the person who expresses rage."[1]

Anger takes at least two forms. The first one is aggressive—like the guy who attacked his car with the lug wrench. The second is passive-aggressive. It's the inner, soul-simmering anger that festers. Aggressive anger is easy to spot. Its manifestations include verbal attacks, name-calling, sarcasm, cursing, ridicule, and physical violence. People with aggressive anger may swing a punch or throw, kick, or smash something. Or they may just stand and scream.

- When was the last time you screamed at someone? How did he or she react?
- How did you feel when it was over? Did you lose the relationship or repair it?

Aggressive anger may take the form of constant negativity—perpetual criticism toward everyone and everything. Negative people may belittle their spouse, children, friends, and co-workers, making them feel they can't do anything right.

Passive-aggressive anger is harder to detect. My father was a cook in the Air Force and liked to make special meals for us. One time he made a blueberry cobbler. It looked delicious on the stove. The top had a great crust and was covered with just the right amount of sugar. But he left it on the burner too long, and we didn't know that until we dug in with our spoons. The interior, all burnt and black, had turned to paste. That's what passive-aggressive anger can do. On the surface you may look fine, but underneath your insides are scorched.

Passive-aggressive anger may show up as self-sabotage or even self-destruction. You inflict feelings of anger on yourself. Instead of moving forward, you get in the way of your own success and enjoyment of life. You may even sabotage the happiness of others. Instead of openly discussing your problems with them or your anger toward them, you try to sabotage their success or happiness. Anger turned inward may also appear as isolation and withdrawal where anger is used to create barriers with others, such as avoidance, refusal to engage in new situations. Anger can also result in depression, perpetual sadness, listlessness, or hopelessness.

People with an anger problem may not realize their emotion is anger. Not all anger is expressed as rage. Because they blame their anger on someone or something else, they don't realize they have the power to change their situation. For example, the guy who was beating his car with his tire tool—he only had to step away and find a better wrench. Then he could have successfully removed his tire. Instead, he acted out his frustration and pounded the car to a pulp—perhaps because he thought, *It's the car's fault.*

In my thirty years of pastoring, I've learned many lessons. One of those lessons can improve every relationship by one hundred percent. With every problem, you have the ability to say, "It's my responsibility to fix this"—because as long as it's someone else's problem, how can it get any better for you? And while you may not be able to physically fix it, as long as you blame it on someone else, it will not get any better.

Every one of us will be challenged by situations that provoke us to anger, and all of us have certain things that set us off more easily than other things might. For instance, for some, the anger trigger might be poor service in a restaurant, while for others it might be disrespectful comments. We might be able to tolerate many things well, but those particular areas really push our buttons. Recognizing anger triggers is a great tool.

Anger triggers can include:

- Threat (we feel "under attack" from someone or something)
- Embarrassment (when someone laughs at us or ridicules us in front of others)
- Rejection (we pour our heart out to someone and they reject us)
- Fatigue (we're tired and can't take one more thing someone asks of us)
- Frustration (due to aggravation, we lose control and want to harm someone or something)

The Bible also warns about the problems of anger. In Job 5:2, Eliphaz said, "For wrath kills a foolish man, and envy slays a simple one." Proverbs 19:19 explains, "A man of great wrath will suffer punishment; for if you rescue him, you will have to do it again." James 1:19 says, "My dear brothers and sisters, take note of this: Everyone should be quick to listen, slow to speak and slow to get angry" (NIV). In Romans 7:21–24 it says,

> I have discovered this principle of life—that when I want to do what is right, I inevitably do what is wrong. I love God's law with all my heart. But there is another power within me that is at war with my mind. This power makes me a slave to the sin that is still within me. Oh, what a miserable person I am! Who will free me from this life that is dominated by sin and death? (NLT)

According to the Bible, we have a natural anger component. Yet anger is not in itself sinful. In fact, it is possible to be angry and not sin. How do we know this? Because Jesus himself felt anger and he was without sin. Anger triggers are threat, embarrassment, rejection, fatigue, frustration—and are all understandable. However, when these emotions become rage, anger doesn't seek to reconcile. It seeks to destroy the person or object causing the anger, resulting in sin.

Let's take a look at nine simple steps for dealing with anger in a constructive way.

Own your anger. Say, "It's mine. Not my spouse's. Not my child's. Not my friend's. Not my colleague's. It's mine."

Process anger. Scripture says, "Let not the sun go down upon your wrath" (Eph. 4:26 KJV). Some people say "sleep on it," but anger is one thing that you don't want to sleep on. Tomorrow is not a guarantee. You need to settle it now—not later.

Express anger in a healthy way. Try expressing your anger in this formula: say to the other person, "Whenever you do (fill in the blank), I feel (fill in the blank), and that makes me (fill in the blank)." When you say this, you are admitting what you feel, but framing it in a rational way.

Control your response. We can't always control where our emotion comes from, or where and how it shows up—but we can control how we respond to it. When you understand that the places *where* you are can affect your thoughts, you can change *how* you think, which will change *what* you think. And when you change what you think, you change your life.

Release anger. After anger is processed and expressed, make sure it is released. This is a great feeling. Resentment is too often cherished in our lives. Somebody hurt us, and we're going to make them pay for it, and we hold on to this for years! Instead, learn to let go of the petty stuff. The only person resentment hurts is you.

Spiritualize it. Make the irritation a matter of prayer.

Get it out of your system. Explain negative feelings to a mature third party. Go meet with someone and say, "This is really making me angry. I'm really upset that this is happening." Get a neutral take on the situation, not from your gossip pal but from a mature person with whom you can talk openly and receive constructive feedback.

Forgive those who have offended you. Harboring resentment is like swallowing poison and expecting your enemy to die. Remember that God allows some frustrations and negative events in our lives to develop our patience and help us grow. Those who learn to handle setbacks develop strength in character.

Remember the forgiveness available in Christ. Remember that nothing anyone does to us can equal the offenses for which God has already forgiven us. What you and I have been forgiven of is so far beyond anything that anybody else is doing to annoy us or hurt us. We need to forgive them and move on.

Exercise

What are triggers that make you lose it? Write them down. Are they people, places, or things? Write down three ways to control your anger. Write three times when you successfully controlled your anger. For more, see Proverbs 16:32, 1 Samuel 20:30, and Proverbs 14:29.

"The thing we fear, we bring to pass."
—Elbert Hubbard

Note

[1]Randy Rowland, *The Sins We Love* (New York: Doubleday, 2000), 86.

Chapter Four

FOCUS ON FEAR

The opposite of love is not hate but fear. Fear will sabotage your relationships.

Relationships are tricky. Even the best relationship must overcome hidden dangers such as anger, gossip, or betrayal. These dangers can poison any connection between two people. However, one danger that is often overlooked is fear. Many overlook ways fear can poison their relationships until it is too late.

There's a multi-billion dollar industry that preys on fear. There are millions of books and thousands of movies all designed to scare us. While I am troubled for weeks when I see one of these movies, that is not the type of fear that I am referring to. I am talking about the *real* fears which cripple and limit our lives. Max Lucado said of fear:

> His *modus operandi* is to manipulate you with the mysterious, to taunt you with the unknown. Fear of death, fear of failure, fear of God, fear of tomorrow—his arsenal is vast. His goal? To create cowardly, joyless souls. He doesn't want you to make the journey to the mountain. He figures if he can rattle you enough, you will take your eyes off the peaks and settle for a dull existence in the flatlands.[1]

This beautiful, lyrical language is all true. Many of us are settling for the flatlands in our relationship with God because we are afraid to go up the mountain. Some of us settle for the lowlands of relationships with our mates, children, or friends because we are scared. It may not even be a terrifying kind of fear—but rather a gnawing, anxious kind of fear. Let's take a closer look at the types of fear that may be causing danger in your relationships.

Fear is the greatest limiter in life. If you have a problem with fear, you will live two lives—one for the approval of others and the other for the real, inner you. If you have a problem with fear, you don't share who you really are with friends and acquaintances for fear of rejection.

Perhaps your friends are conservative in their politics and you find that you disagree on certain issues. You don't express your disagreement out of fear that they might like you less. Inside, you feel strongly about a progressive issue, but you allow your silence on the discussion to convince your conservative friends that you feel the same as they do. So there is the private-you that feels one way, and the public-you that keeps silent and denies your beliefs out of the fear of rejection.

Another type of fear may cause you to attack innocent emotional patterns displayed by your mate or friends because it triggers memories of negative patterns from significant people in your past. Let me give you an example. In a group meeting I had recently, a woman shared that fear had a significant impact on her relationship with her husband. Her mother-in-law was a master manipulator and manipulated her son all the time. When she wanted him to do something, she would always use guilt to trick him. She would cry and indicate that she might be dead when he got back from spending time with his friends.

While the woman's husband was younger, his mother's behavior worked, but as he aged he grew to resent it. The problem was that when he and his wife had a real issue and she began to cry, he went ballistic! He could not have the discussion because he was afraid his wife was trying to manipulate him the way his mother did. In this way, fear can cause us to manipulate and attack what are often innocent emotional patterns of loved ones because of the memories they trigger.

Fear can also hold us back from life. A family may resist opportunities for promotion because they fear change. A parent may be afraid to love a child for fear she may someday leave. Someone may resist her spouse's successes or sabotage his efforts because she fears if he has the means to leave, he will.

We also see this kind of fear surface when one partner who has been overweight makes significant lifestyle changes and sheds unwanted pounds. Sometimes the man will sabotage his wife's efforts by bringing home candy and other sweets while she is in the middle of a diet. Or he may create roadblocks to her exercise program by overscheduling their commitments. At the core of this behavior is his fear that if she becomes more attractive, she won't be able to resist any men who flirt with her and will leave him. This is a sad scenario because often the wife who is making changes wants to do so to please her husband and would never think of hurting him. Fear leads some to sabotage the plans of the person they love the most.

Some people may even withhold love from others. They fear that if people know how much they love them, they will use it to manipulate them and gain control. I have known several men who had a strange belief that they needed to keep their mate a little insecure in the relationship or else they would be dominated and controlled by their lover. I suppose they had seen a negative example of someone manipulating their spouse in the past and had absorbed this belief. One person said to me, "The one who cares the most in a relationship is the one in the weakest position." That may be a sound strategy for negotiating to buy a car—not showing how much you want the vehicle—but it's a terrible formula for a marriage or any other deep relationship.

The depth of our communication is another area where fear can cause us to withhold our love. A person may keep all conversations on a surface level and never talk about real life problems in relationships for fear they cannot handle the outcomes of those discussions.

Maybe one person in the relationship fears that the other is losing interest in him. Instead of bringing the subject up and talking it through, he will keep silent out of fear of what might be said when he begins the discussion. What if his lover says, "Yes, I am getting bored with the relationship," or some other complaint? This is a foolish strategy because many of our fears in relationships are misunderstandings and once something is brought to the light in discussion, it is easy to remove false and painful assumptions. I think there is great wisdom in the phrase, "When in doubt, check it out."

I knew one couple in which the husband would tell his spouse that he was depressed and was contemplating suicide. This kind of talk terrified his young wife and she would be filled with panic if her husband was late coming home or could not be reached by phone. She never said anything because she was afraid it would make him even more depressed. One day, she mustered her courage and told him how deeply upsetting his threats to harm himself were to her. Her husband was surprised that she had taken him so seriously as he had merely been letting off steam in a thoughtless manner. He was chagrined that he had caused his wife, whom he loved dearly, such pain. He immediately apologized and never again threatened suicide. What is sad is that the wife endured several years of needless pain by allowing fear to keep her from talking about a difficult subject.

Other ways fear can affect relationships: You may refuse to enter into appealing new relationships for fear of repeating negative patterns from the past. You don't say what you want or ask for what you want or need in relationships for fear of rejection. You live small because you fear taking responsibility for living large.

Fear may cause you to attempt to control your mate's friends, work life, and finances because you are afraid others may find him or her attractive. God is always kept at arm's length because you fear what he may ask you to do. Many a believer has resisted a deeper walk with God out of fear that God may send them to a foreign country as missionaries or ask some other difficult task of them. They are forgetting, of course, that God will always create a desire within you for any challenge he calls you to take. I've known hundreds of missionaries personally, and all of them testify that they love what they do and feel blessed to be called to serve in the countries God has led them to. You may take on fixing others' burdens and messes for fear you might have contributed to or caused their mistakes. Fear may prevent you from saying, "I'm sorry," because you may be perceived as weak. Some parents are even overly suspicious of their children's behavior for fear they will repeat mistakes they made in their youth.

- Do you try to control others' finances, work life, or friends? Do you fear if others like them, they will leave you?
- Do you have any hidden fears that are hurting your relationships?
- What can you do to overcome these fears?

Fear can have a profound impact on our behavior and relationships. I'm sure you can recognize one or two of those behaviors. Fear has been present through the ages, including in the Bible. Let's look at some biblical examples of fear and how it affects relationships.

In Genesis 21, Sarah was afraid that her husband, Abraham, loved her handmaiden, Hagar, more because they had produced a son together named Ishmael. Sarah drove Ishmael away and drove Hagar out of the camp, even though she was the one who started the relationship between Hagar and Abraham so he could have a son.

Fear shattered the home of Isaac and his wife Rebekah later in Genesis. They had two sons who were twins: Esau and Jacob. Rebekah loved Jacob the most, and Isaac loved Esau the most. However, both were afraid that their favor for one child would result in neglect of the other. Their home was emotionally destroyed by that fear.

In the New Testament, we see that Peter had a jealous fear of John the Beloved after the resurrection. Peter said to Jesus in fear, "What shall this man do?" (John 21:21 KJV). He did not understand that it didn't matter what Jesus did with someone else. It doesn't matter what Jesus does with other Christians, it only matters to you what Jesus does with *you*. Yet many in the Bible feared to approach God. Their fear was that sin had irrevocably damaged the relationship. For example, the rich young ruler who went running, kneeling, and falling at the feet of Jesus said, "What must I do to inherit eternal life?" (Mark 10:17 NIV). In Galatians 2:1–14, the Apostle Peter feared the rejection of Jewish Christians. This in turn caused him to snub the Gentile Christians with whom he had formerly shared meals.

Like the biblical people of old, many people are still afraid to approach God because of their sins and past failings. Some things may even seem unforgivable to them. Yet they don't understand: those who fear God's rejection misunderstand God's nature. We need to know the heart of God. God loves us *so* much, there is *nothing* we can do, will do, or ever even think of doing that will cause him to stop loving us or prevent his forgiveness. Do not ever be afraid to run to God when you need him. There is no reason to turn away when we are struggling, because God will always be there for us.

It would be a pretty bleak picture if there were not ways to overcome our fears. Turn to God in the midst of struggles. And here is some additional advice: if you are struggling with fear, inspect your beliefs. You fear because you think something, and you think something because you believe something. So inspect what you believe. What is true about the things you believe? It may not be biblical beliefs and spiritual beliefs that are causing fear; it may be how you think of your wife, your husband, and your friends and how they react. Let me explain further.

Most of our beliefs are generalizations about our past. We've all had certain things happen, and then we generalize about them. Often, our beliefs are based on misinterpretations of past experiences. It takes a really mature person to examine things and say, "Is this *really* truth? Or is this just what someone told me?" The Bible encourages us to examine ourselves and see whether or not we are "in the faith" (2 Cor. 13:5). Open your mind and look at your faith and see if you *really* have a relationship with God. Do you *really* know God? Do you *really* understand the Scriptures? Do you read Scripture with an open mind? Do you understand biblical truths? Or are you just regurgitating something someone told you when you were young? Is it truth or is it trash? It is important to reexamine our beliefs as adults to make sure we were taught and accepted correct values and beliefs.

You need to challenge your beliefs in order to make sure they are based on the truth.

- Do I really have a personal relationship with God?
- Do I *really* know God? Do I truly understand the Scriptures?
- Do I think God is satisfied with my relationship with him?

Another way to overcome fear is to recognize that negative events in our lives can materialize from that fear. Sometimes, if you fear something enough it can become reality. The patriarch Job said, "For the thing I greatly feared has come upon me, and what I dreaded has happened to me" (Job 3:25).

When I was a kid, we went to youth camp. We had about thirty hormonal teenagers on the bus, and the leaders were all scared to death that our behavior would be wild. One summer, a camp director said, "Here you're not going to do this, you're not going to do that! And, oh! You better not be thinking that, you better not be trying to sneak around and do that, and most of all you better not try to ring the bell in the middle of the camp. There is a big bell and it's for dinner, and don't you *dare* think about ringing that bell!" Wherever he learned psychology, he learned a bad tactic. Guess what we did the first night and every night thereafter? *We rang that bell!* When you fear something negative, it can become reality.

Another year at the same camp, we had a different director. He got on the bus and said in front of our group of teenagers, "I expect you to act like the adults you are. I expect you to be the Christians you are. You have good morals, and I know you have good intentions. This is going to be a good spiritual week. I know that I can count on you to behave in a good manner." Now, were we the perfect youth? No, but we behaved better than we had with the first camp director, and it was because our leader didn't anticipate negative behavior.

Another way to control fear is to accept that everything worth doing involves a certain amount of risk. Progress always involves risk. You can't steal second base with your foot firmly planted on first. Take action in the areas of your fear. Or in the words of Ralph Waldo Emerson, "Do the thing you fear and the death of fear is certain."

Do you remember going on the high dive for the first time at the swimming pool when you were a kid? Do you remember the mixture of excitement and fear as you ran up to get in line? I remember I got to where I could jump off the low dive, but all those other people were going up on the high dive, and I wanted to go on the high dive, but it was *high*! When you are only four feet tall, sixteen feet is a long way up. I remember going up the ladder and changing my mind at the top a couple of times. It was just *too high*! I remember finally going all the way up the ladder and looking off the edge of the board. It was a long way down! But eventually I made myself take the leap and here's what I learned. You struggle with the fear and weigh the risk, but finally you work past the fear and jump off, and you survive. Wow! And then you are going back for a second time!

If you do the thing you fear, the power of that fear goes away. This applies to our relationships as well. Are you afraid to ask God for what you really want? Are you afraid of having a certain conversation with your parents or your children? If you do the thing you fear, that fear will vanish.

Examine the opportunities lost if we don't face our fears. If you are afraid of telling a spouse your feelings, look at the lost opportunity if you don't tell that person your fears. How much is it costing you because you are not being honest? Be strong and take action in the areas of your fears. Make sure you don't create negative images or thoughts, and accept that everything worth doing includes a risk. Look at the lost opportunities if we don't face our fears and inspect our beliefs—each one is a cure for fear.

The best cure of all for fear is faith. We master fear through faith. As we incorporate faith into our lives, fear vanishes: As believers in Christ, what is our heritage? "For God has not given us a spirit of fear, but of power and of love and of a sound mind" (2 Tim. 1:7). That is, if we feel fear, it is not coming from God. He gave us power and love and a sound mind. That's the greatest power for overcoming fear. Faith overcomes our fear. That's why it's so wonderful to be a Christian. I love being a Christian for lots of reasons, but one of the greatest of them is the benefit of overcoming fear.

- If we are feeling fear, does it come from God?
- What powers does God give us to fight fear?

Let's examine the other benefits of being a Christian. In the book of Colossians, Paul talks about what Christ has done for our sins. Think about what shames you to your core and then realize what God did with that.

> And you, being dead in your trespasses and the uncircumcision of your flesh, He has made alive together with Him, having forgiven you all trespasses, having wiped out the handwriting of requirements that was against us, which was contrary to us. And He has taken it out of the way, having nailed it to the cross. (Col. 2:13–14)

He has forgiven all our sins and taken them out of the way.

"For you did not receive the spirit of bondage again to fear, but you received the Spirit of adoption by whom we cry out, 'Abba, Father.' The Spirit Himself bears witness with our spirit that we are children of God" (Rom. 8:15–16). In Christ I am not just forgiven, but he has invited me in, and he has adopted me into his family. How long will God forgive our sins and adopt us into his family? Again, we read in the Bible, "Do not grieve the Holy Spirit of God, by whom you were sealed for the day of redemption" (Eph. 4:30). If you can, think of yourself as a package that's going to be delivered to heaven, and your soul is in that package; the Spirit has sealed you for eternity. It's a guarantee of delivery.

Now, if you know you are forgiven of your sins, that you've been made part of God's family and that you're sealed for eternity, what is there to be afraid of? It doesn't make any sense to have fear. Since you're forgiven, adopted, and sealed, you can relax in your relationship with God. Quit waiting for God to get disgusted with you. Stop waiting for God to have enough of you, because he never will! You can love him and always go to him with your problems.

What happens when we sin is that we run *away* from God instead of running *to* him—perhaps it is from guilt or shame. That is a trick of Satan. Instead, we should run *to* him because we are adopted, sealed, and forgiven. The security of God is needed to fearlessly examine our fears.

Because you are forgiven, adopted, and sealed, what's the worst that could happen if you tried that thing you've always been afraid of? Fear is a terrible limiter. It limits you from walking with God, growing in faith, building your relationships, and a hundred other things. Use the security of your relationship with God to destroy fear in your life.

Exercises

1. Choose something that you've always been afraid of and confront it. If you have a fear of snakes, visit the reptile house at the zoo and force yourself to look at every exhibit.
2. Make a commitment to discuss with your spouse something that you have been annoyed by but have been avoiding talking about.
3. Deliberately put yourself in an uncomfortable situation just to show yourself that you probably had exaggerated fears about how bad it would be.

"The glory of Christianity is to conquer by forgiveness."
—William Blake

Note

[1]Max Lucado, *The Applause of Heaven* (Nashville: Thomas Nelson, 1990), 78.

Chapter Five

ADDICTION TO THE PAST

Good, bad, or ugly, the past is gone.
Unless you can release your past,
your relationships will never flourish.

How many of us live in the past? Or even worse, how many are under the misapprehension that we can never change the past? Perhaps our past life was happier than the one we now have. Some may even fantasize about the past to avoid facing the realities of today. Or, as is most often the case, perhaps there are things in our past that were terrible that we wish we'd done differently. An unhealthy relationship with the past—an addiction to the past—prevents many from having healthy relationships in the present and future.

Writing in Philippians, Paul says, "Brethren, I do not count myself to have apprehended; but one thing I do, forgetting those things which are behind and reaching forward to those things which are ahead, I press toward the goal for the prize of the upward call of God in Christ Jesus" (Phil. 3:13–14). Paul means that he hasn't attained perfection, and he hasn't gotten it all together yet, but he is able to forget those things which are behind him. The principle in this verse is powerful and is that you can't move forward if you remain mired in the past. Being stuck in the past is a hidden danger that prevents us from having healthy relationships today.

Many people face an addiction to the past. *Addiction* is a strong word to use, and many will say, "Well, I'm familiar with the past, or I like the past, but addiction?" Yet, if you think about it, sometimes people find comfort in the past like an addict seeks comfort with his or her drug of choice. People turn to it to get them out of the present moment. They turn to the past so they don't have to focus on what's going on in their lives *right now*. So many of us focus on or idealize the past because it is safe. They say "the past is behind us," but it's not really safe and harmless if it prevents us from living today.

Someone once said, "The past is a valuable guidepost, but it's dangerous if it's used as a hitching post." It's okay to reference the past—it's silly not to—but if you are defined by it, and it keeps you from becoming the person you could be today, then the past is dangerous.

What might addiction to the past look like in a relationship? I'm going to give you some suggestions. Your disagreements might always circle around past mistakes and failures. Each time you have a discussion or disagreement, no matter what the subject, you dredge up past problems. I know a couple who, every time they got in an argument, would end up fighting about what happened on their honeymoon. The honeymoon was *twenty-five years* ago! It didn't matter if they were upset about the grocery bill from an hour ago—sooner or later they would work it all the way back to what happened on their honeymoon. That is seriously damaging to a relationship.

Perhaps you are frustrated with trying to build a great relationship with your spouse because you are fixated on past relationships; you have trouble loving the person your spouse has become. You only remember what he or she once was. You don't trust your loved ones today because loved ones in the past hurt you deeply. You blame your failures in life on your parents, or your teachers, or the church, or anybody else's failure to raise you the right way. You think or act out the idea of, "You know it's not my fault! It was my dad, it was my mom, or it was the church. I'm not sure who is at fault; I'm just sure it's not my fault."

An addiction to memories of good times past keeps you from enjoying life today. You can't do anything new in your life because you've always done things a certain way. You drive the same way to work, drive the same kind of vehicle, and wear the same kind of clothes because you've always done it that way. You can't go to new places when you travel because you have to return to the ones where you used to go.

Are you the type that won't let yourself off the hook for past failures in life? That's a lot of us. You must punish yourself because no one else has and you feel deserving of punishment. We need to remember that as Christians, we've been forgiven in Jesus Christ; his blood flowed and his mercy was shown. If he has forgiven you and put your sins behind him to remember them no more, why do you keep bringing them up?

- Do you wear the same type of clothing because that is what you *always* wear?
- Do you drive a certain type of vehicle because that's what you drove in the past?
- Are you repeating any other behaviors because that is what you did in the past?
- Does it anger you when people suggest updating your look or home?

The dedication to the memories of your husband or wife is so strong that you live in bondage to their past preferences. You define yourself by labels. You say things like, "I'm the strong silent type," as opposed to learning to open up and talk to your mate about your feelings. When it comes to changing your diet, you hide behind the label of "weak" instead of putting in the work to strengthen your resistance to temptations because you failed at previous attempts. It's easier to label yourself than to work for change. You won't let your children forget the sacrifices you made for them. You won't let your children grow into who they could become because you don't want to miss who they were.

Let's look at some biblical examples of focusing on the past. Think about the nation of Israel. They had been slaves in Egypt for a long time and prayed to God for deliverance. God sent Moses, and he delivered them through the ten plagues on the Egyptians, and they marched out into the desert, free, singing songs of praises to God. But after they had been out in the wilderness for a little while, and they had to eat the same food every day, they got tired of it and became ungrateful. Numbers 11:5 says that they began to long for the foods and spices in Egypt. They said to Moses, "Oh, we miss the leeks and the garlic of Egypt." They told Moses they'd had it good back in Egypt. But they forgot—they were wearing chains and building the pyramids! They were slaves in Egypt! What a powerful example of people addicted to the past.

Consider the Jewish leaders who could not accept Jesus as the Messiah because he did not fit their pattern of the past. Can you imagine being a religious leader around Jesus and having the audacity to say to Christ, the Son of God, "I don't like the way you wash your hands before we eat"? And then going on:

> You don't wash your hands the way we have ritually washed our hands, and every good teacher knows that there is a certain way that you are supposed to wash your hands before you eat. And Jesus—you just don't fit that pattern. I don't care that you can walk on water and that you raised Lazarus from the dead. I don't care that blind people can see; you don't know how to wash your hands, so I do not believe in you.

That's exactly what happened. They could not accept Jesus as their Messiah because he did not fit their pattern of the past.

Then we have the New Testament Jewish Christians. They were new converts to a new faith with roots in Judaism. They accepted Christ as their Savior, but they kept trying to drag Gentiles (non-Jews) back into the observance of old Jewish rituals and holy days, saying, "I know we're Christians; I know Christ is the Messiah, but we used to do it this way; we used to have the feast of Yom Kippur; we used to have this and we still need to do those things." We are warned of this behavior in the following verses: "Do you wish to be enslaved by them all over again?" (Gal. 4:9 NIV). "Anyone who belongs to Christ has become a new person" (2 Cor. 5:17 NLT). "It is no longer I who live, but Christ lives in me" (Gal. 2:20). We are not under bondage to the past.

Then consider the church at Jerusalem, which had trouble accepting Paul as an apostle of the church because they had such a strong memory of him as "Saul the persecutor." Before Paul became the Apostle Paul, he persecuted Christians. His name was Saul. Then he had an encounter with God that transformed him. He became a Christian and it turned his life upside down. Saul became a preacher of the gospel, and God changed his name to Paul. However, when he went to Jerusalem, ready to help and ready to worship, they said, "No, we know who you are!" They could only view him as Saul. Stuck in the past, they couldn't accept his new identity. It took Barnabas, a respected leader in the church, to stand up to them and say that he had changed—that he was not who he used to be (Acts 9:27).

Why is it so foolish to focus on the past? Well, to start with, the past is gone. It's not coming back. Someone once said, "You can't ride a wave that went out yesterday." Another reason focusing on the past is foolish is that our memory plays tricks. It chooses to remember and omit certain things. You may not remember *exactly* what once was. The mind often remembers the good and forgets the bad.

The freed Israelites did this exact thing when they looked back on their time in Egypt. They forgot about their murdered children and that they were beaten with whips. People still do that today. We wish we could go back to when we were in our prime. It is human nature to look back and remember the good times. That's the way God made our brains, to remember the good and forget the bad. Retaining every bad memory would make us sick. As a result, we get this nostalgia for the good old days.

Not long ago, I was teasing a friend about how much summer youth camp costs today. I told him that the first time I went to camp, it cost only twenty-five dollars and that we had a wonderful time. In my memory, it was a great camp. While I recalled a good time, I was forgetting some of the uncomfortable things about that camp. The church drove us to the campsite in a '62 Chevrolet bus with no air conditioning. It was *hot*. We stayed in dorms that didn't have air conditioning and had concrete floors and mosquitoes that pestered us all night long! The plumbing didn't work half of the time, and the food was the most awful food you ever had in your life. The worship services took place in an old, open-air tabernacle where the temperature felt about one hundred eighty degrees Fahrenheit. I told him it was a good time, but the truth was only some of it was good. Our memories often downplay the bad and highlight the positive.

It is dangerous to fixate on the past because it limits your joy and the joy of others. People often use tradition, whether it's a tradition in the church or a tradition in their family, to manipulate others. I once heard a man say, "I don't have to work hard at growing our relationship. My wife is always complaining that I don't give compliments, but in our family we never have. So she'll just have to get used to it." What did he mean? That's just the way it is? What a ridiculous attitude. Blaming bad habits on tradition is never a good excuse.

- What are the dangers of living in the past?
- How has focusing on the past hurt your spiritual growth?
- Is your prayer life stuck at the same level it was twenty years ago?

Why is the past so dangerous? Because looking at the past can be dangerous to your spiritual life. There are times when it is beneficial to look back—it is an encouragement to see how far God has brought us in our spiritual growth and to marvel at his provision in past trials. But there is a kind of looking back that is dangerous. Believers can be deceived into looking back at their lives before Christ if they look unwisely. Those who become Christians later in life sometimes will look back and say, "Man, you know I had some good times when I was young. There were times when it was great." But we are warned in Scripture when the Lord spoke, "No one, having put his hand to the plow, and looking back, is fit for the kingdom of God" (Luke 9:62). God doesn't want us looking back at the past if what we are looking at is our enjoyment of sins. He wants us looking to the future. Looking back in the wrong manner will stunt our spiritual growth.

Hebrews 6:1 teaches that, as believers, people tend to remain stuck in the entry levels of spiritual life. Sometimes the past makes us feel that if we've read this book of the Bible or completed this spiritual course, then we've arrived. Yet the Bible tells us we're to be moving forward constantly. One translation of this powerful verse in Hebrews says, "So let us stop going over the basic teachings about Christ again and again. Let us go on instead and become mature in our understanding" (Heb. 6:1 NLT). It's not that we can't repeat the basics when needed, but once we get the basics down, it is important to move forward in spiritual growth. Do we want to be stuck at the same level of Christian growth now as we were last year, or even years ago?

Sometimes people want to retell the stories of what they did for Christ in the past. And while it's great to know what you once did for God, the more exciting question is: What are you doing for God *right now*?

- Do you ever repeat to others what you have done for God *in the past*?
- What have you done for God *today*?

So what is the best way to overcome an addiction to the past? Well, many people have issues of real emotional pain. Sometimes there are things so painful that people don't want to reference them at all. That's okay and I understand that fear. After a great deal of thought and prayer, I've come up with some basic ideas. For those who don't have such deep aggravations in your past, I hope they will push you forward into the future. Others may need more perspective or counseling. Let's consider what can be done to release the past.

What is the only thing that can be done about the past? Face it honestly, and change your response to it. The past cannot be changed, but our response to it can. That is really the only thing you can do. That wave already went out. Those parents are gone. That relationship has ended. That job opportunity will never come again. You can't go back, but you can change your response to it. You can change how you are letting it affect you today. How? Put the past in perspective. Remember, you view the past with the eyes of a lesser person than you are today. When you look at the past and some aggravation you had there, perhaps something that happened when you were a child or a teenager, that's the lens you see the experience through.

When I was a teenager, I had a terrible experience with rejection. That experience caused a great deal of emotional pain. It involved a lovely young girl. She was in my English class when we were in high school. Let's just call her Debbie. I thought she was the most beautiful creature in the world. She was a popular cheerleader. I desperately wanted Debbie to talk to me. So, in spite of being socially inept, I worked up the courage to approach her in the hall one day.

At six foot three inches and 127 pounds, struggling with acne and a shy personality, I approached her when she was surrounded by a crowd of kids. I tapped her on the shoulder and said, "Hi, Debbie!" and she turned around and said, "Eeeww, I don't like you," and she slapped me. She *slapped* me in front of that entire crowd! I must have surprised her or she was being silly, but she slapped me and laughed. I was mortally embarrassed and quickly covered my face and walked away. It was a devastating experience, and I was wounded by it for a long time.

However, to overcome the past, I must make a point *not* to remember that experience as a teenage boy. I'm not a fourteen-year-old boy any longer, and I can put it in a different perspective now. I can say: "That was a silly teenage girl. That was a fourteen-year-old child who did a silly thing without knowing what impact it would have." When I think of it that way, the pain flows out of me and is easier to forgive.

When you look at the past, remember that you're looking at it with the eyes of who you were then, but that's not who you are now. Force yourself to see the pain of the past through the eyes of the mature person you are today.

- Do you have a painful past experience that is hard to release?
- Are you a different person now than you were then?
- What would happen if you viewed that experience through your current perspective, and not through the eyes of the inexperienced person you were then?

Release your relationships from the tyranny of the past. Your relationships today may be suffering from what happened to you in the past. Quit arguing about what you did on the honeymoon. Stop fussing about something that happened to you when you were sixteen! Determine to approach troubled relationships as if there were no preexisting conditions. When you need to have a difficult discussion, determine to approach it as if it were the very first time you were having a conversation with that person. This technique will give you new power in your relationships.

Realize that if you are a believer in Christ, you are connected to the one who is timeless. That is why it is *so good* to be a Christian. This is one of the many benefits of knowing Jesus as your Savior. When you come to know Christ, you become a joint heir with Jesus who is timeless. To paraphrase the beautiful Colossians 1:27, it is now "Christ who is *in* you, the hope of glory." He will be with you *right now* to help you process the change you need to make. Aren't you glad you are connected to an eternal God?

Another way to look at it is that the life you will have in an eternity with Christ is actually a part of your experience of life today. It means that you can, in this present moment and with the help of the Holy Spirit, be the kind of person that you are going to be when the kingdom of heaven is realized here on earth. The logic is this: because he's in me, I'm able to be the perfected creature in Christ now that I one day will be for all eternity. So what does that mean to our past? It means to let go of the past because whatever it was, it is no longer. As a child of God, you've got something glorious in front of you. You are a glorious creature becoming ever more glorious every day.

I once read a quote from C. S. Lewis concerning the future appearance of people when they take on their true, unearthly forms:

> It is a serious thing to live in a society of possible gods and goddesses, to remember that the dullest most uninteresting person you can talk to may one day be a creature which, if you saw it now, you would be strongly tempted to worship, or else a horror and a corruption such as you now meet, if at all, only in a nightmare.[1]

If it's true that in Christ I am already a creature so incredible that others might be tempted to worship me, then why am I dragging around all of this junk from the past as if I were stuck with it?

Don't let the past run your life today. It's behind you and it's gone. You are preparing for eternity. The Christian life that we live, we now live by faith. We live it in preparation for the world to come. We are being prepared to rule and reign with Christ. That means that the challenges you had in your past and the challenges you have in the present all have a purpose. That purpose is to shape you into the person you are going to be in eternity. The process of becoming more like Christ is one of the main reasons for letting go of the past, so that you can become who you were meant to be. Have you ever thought about how your addiction to past feelings and thoughts keeps you from becoming what you should be?

William Barclay wrote a commentary called *The Daily Study Bible.* In an explanation of 2 Corinthians 6:11–13, he tells a story about a man and one of the great regrets of his life. It occurred when he was a young boy. This man and some friends went to a crossing of two major roads, and they switched the direction signs for the roads. This was before navigation systems and GPS. People depended on those signs to find the way to their destinations. People, not knowing that the signs had been tampered with, no doubt went many miles in the wrong direction.

Barclay writes that years later when this man was on his deathbed, when he thought of all those people going the wrong way because of what he had done, he was still crushed by it. How great a responsibility is it to send someone on a false path? Have you ever caused people to go the wrong way? Isn't that a powerful thought? If so, we can't go back and undo what we've done. All we can do is say to ourselves, "I can change my response to that past action."

How do you change a response to a past action? Understand that you are not the same person you were when you acted improperly. Even in those experiences, God had a purpose. He had a lesson to teach in that behavior, a lesson that could not have been learned any other way. It is only by the grace of God that we move forward. I hope you are courageous enough to let go of the past and move into your glorious future.

Exercise

When do you tend to get stuck in the past? Write down three examples. Next, write three ways to change your response to the past. Practice living in the present. Start today. For more, see Luke 9:62, James 1:6–8, and Ephesians 2:1–8.

"It is wonderful how much time good people spend fighting the devil. If they would only expend the same amount of energy loving their fellow men, the devil would die in his own tracks of ennui."
—Helen Keller

Notes

[1]C. S. Lewis, *The Weight of Glory* (New York: Harper Press, 2001), 45.

[2]William Barclay, *The Daily Study Bible: The Letters to the Corinthians* (Philadelphia: West Minister Press, 1975), 219.

Chapter Six

LACK OF SPIRITUAL DIRECTION

Learn how to tap into the hidden benefits of spirituality.

> Oh, taste and see that the Lord is good; blessed is the man who trusts in Him! Oh, fear the Lord, you His saints! There is no want to those who fear Him. The young lions lack and suffer hunger; but those who seek the Lord shall not lack any good thing. Come, you children, listen to me; I will teach you the fear of the Lord. Who is the man who desires life, and loves many days, that he may see good? Keep your tongue from evil, and your lips from speaking deceit. Depart from evil and do good; seek peace and pursue it. (Ps. 34:8–14)

When I was a teenager, my most prized possession was my 1969 fire engine red Ford Mustang. I loved that car, not just because it was beautiful, but also because it was fast. There was nothing I loved more than to find a quiet back road in the country and really open that engine up. I raced down the road, hitting speeds that were mostly legal but definitely pushing the boundaries for my skills and the road conditions.

One day, I had some free time and I spent about an hour tearing up and down a back road and had a marvelous time. Then I went to a local fast food restaurant to eat. When I got out of the car and started toward the front door of the restaurant, something about the front tire of my car caught my eye. I stopped for a closer look and saw a huge bulge on the inside of my tire. My tire had developed a bubble on the inside wall next to the engine. It was obvious that I was very close to a blowout and that this tire was nearly ruined. As I was looking at the tire, I realized that the bulge must have been on the tire the entire time I was racing out in the country. Had that tire blown when I was speeding down those country roads, I would surely have rolled the car and had a terrible wreck. I realized I had been in real danger and didn't even know it.

This is just like the challenges people face in their lives. There are some behaviors that can either ruin or create relationships that people are not aware of until it is too late.

Many people get into trouble from the hidden danger of having a lack of spiritual direction in life. This includes not knowing God, not being connected to the eternal, and not having a solid rock on which to build your life. There is great danger in being spiritually adrift. You can be in a career you love, and for the moment, your relationships with your family and friends seem to be strong. But the fact is, your spiritual life may be adrift. In your spiritual life there are no roots. You might be atheist, agnostic, or not know what to believe in.

What are some of the challenges that arise out of this? What does the lack of spiritual direction look like in a person's life? The things I'm going to talk about don't apply to every person. It's possible to have a healthy, strong life without having a relationship with God. Yet I have observed that, more often than not, those who have not put down their spiritual roots are more vulnerable. If you haven't created a strong relationship with God, you are especially susceptible to poor self-esteem because it's hard to get through life when you don't believe in yourself. It's pretty difficult to love someone else when you don't love yourself. What is a cure for low self-esteem? It is a belief in the concept that you are a divinely created child of God. He calls you his "peculiar treasure." Jesus came, died on the cross, and shed his blood to save you from sin. That's a pretty positive concept that you mean that much to God.

Some people get hung up on the theory of evolution and creation theories. But it doesn't matter because what is real is that God created you. He loved you. He died for you. This is a source of strength and powerful emotion in life. The fact is, if you don't have a life plan and goals for yourself, other people will. There are some pretty nefarious people out there. They want to use you and build a plan for your life where they can take advantage of you. "If you don't stand for something, you'll fall for anything," and there's not only that danger, but there's instability in time of crisis. If you haven't connected to God, it's pretty hard to be strong when life throws you some curveballs. Without roots, how will you stand firm when the floods come?

James tells us,

> If you need wisdom, ask our generous God and he will give it to you. He will not rebuke you for asking. But when you ask him, be sure that your faith is in God alone. Do not waver, for a person with divided loyalty is as unsettled as a wave of the sea that is blown and tossed by the wind. Such people should not expect to receive anything from the Lord. Their loyalty is divided between God and the world, and they are unstable in everything they do. (James 1:5–8 NLT)

If you don't have faith in God, it's hard to be solid. You're going to be unstable in all your ways. There's power in spiritual direction. There's greater vulnerability to the addictions and vices of life if you don't have it. You can dodge a lot of emotional wreckage in your life by building a relationship with God. In addition, people with lack of spiritual direction are less likely to display compassion and grace for the failures of their mates or their children. All relationships require forgiveness. It will be much easier to forgive the ones you care about when you are on a strong spiritual path.

Another area that's dangerous to relationships is when we become vulnerable to the destructive aspects of pride. Relationships can crater due to pride. Do you remember that great old song from country singer Mac Davis, which contained the words: "It's hard to be humble when you're perfect in every way"? I've met people like that. Some folks who are very proud of their driving are really not as good at driving as they think they are. Some people are proud of their cooking or athletic skills, and they have a false sense of their own talent.

Pride is such an easy trap for us. Pride may not seem dangerous, but the Bible says that pride goes before destruction and haughtiness before a fall (Prov. 16:18 NLT). A prideful individual tends toward a judgmental spirit and can sear relationships with the pain of resentment. Remember that Jesus said in the Gospel of Matthew, "Judge not, that you be not judged. . . . And why do you look at the speck in your brother's eye, but do not consider the plank in your own eye?" (Matt. 7:1, 3). Isn't that a powerful metaphor Jesus gave, when he said you've got a two-by-four sticking out of your eye and the other person only has a splinter in his eye, and you think the other person is the one who needs to work on his attitude?

- Have you ever called someone out for a behavior that you need to break?
- Do you criticize others for the same areas you need to work on?

Pride can destroy our relationships. It's hard to admit when you're wrong. I think about a friend of mine who is now in heaven, and his daughter who greatly disappointed him. At twenty, she entered into a relationship with a young man and her father didn't approve. He forbade her to have a relationship with him. After arguing about it, she finally left home. I don't remember the details, but the relationship was severed. A couple of years passed, and she reached out to him. He wanted to reach out to his daughter, but he was still mad and wanted an apology. When she didn't offer one, he refused to reconcile. Thirty more years went by. *Thirty years*!

He became a Christian and his life was transformed. A few weeks later, he heard a sermon on pride, and it changed his heart. He called his daughter and said, "I want to see my grandkids." Luckily, that was a relationship she was willing to rekindle. He came to my office and broke down and said, "I've wasted thirty years of my life because I was proud." I'm telling you that if you don't have a spiritual connection in your life and you don't have a relationship with God, you're susceptible to pride.

Without spiritual direction, your family life can suffer. It can lead to a bad choice of a marriage partner. The Bible warns us,

> Do not be unequally yoked together with unbelievers. . . . As God has said: "I will dwell in them and walk among them. I will be their God, and they shall be My people." Therefore "Come out from among them and be separate, says the Lord. Do not touch what is unclean, and I will receive you. I will be a Father to you, and you shall be My sons and daughters, says the LORD Almighty." (2 Cor. 6:14a, 16b–18)

Don't team up with unbelievers.

Do you want to have better relationships in life? Don't marry someone who doesn't love the Lord like you do. Why not dodge that bullet? For example, there can be strife over how to handle religious instruction. Your family gets to the point where you are ready to bring that first little darling child to Sunday school, but when and where? If mom and dad are not on the same page spiritually, there can be questions about the meaning of life and where we came from. "Who is God and who am I?" Children can have trauma and turmoil if mom and dad are not on the same page. So what can we do? George Eliot said, "It's never too late to be what you might have been." I like that. Let's get started now.

- Should your number one prerequisite for a marriage partner be someone who is spiritually matched with you?
- Have you had this discussion with a potential spouse?
- If you are of different faiths, have you discussed in what religion you want to raise your children?

Take a hard look at problems in your relationships. Is there a problem with friends? Are there issues with your mate or your children? Ask yourself if these difficulties are the result of a poor spiritual alignment with God. *Do you really know God?* If you know God, do you know Christ? If you know Christ, are you living for him? If not, maybe that is the problem and there is a need to turn to God and realign your life. Turn to God for the salvation and the sanity of your life in this world. Karl Menninger was a medical doctor greatly troubled by the state of the world in the 1970s. He said, "We need to turn to God to transcend one's own self-centeredness. . . . It's not a virtue. It's a saving necessity."[1]

When we come to Christ, we commit our behaviors to the teachings of God. I have a friend who is in prison. He receives our church bulletin and said, "People don't seem to care about being a disciple. I'm glad to hear you talking about it." He said that the phrase disciple of Christ came about because Christians were following Christ. They were adhering to his teachings. We should understand that we have to commit to aligning our behaviors with his teachings.

Do you remember the name Gordon Liddy? He was one of the Watergate co-conspirators and went to prison for it. He came to faith very late in life and observed, "Now the hardest thing I have to do every day is figure out what is God's will. What does Jesus want, not what does Gordon want?"

- Are you serious about being a believer?
- Do you find your relationship with God to be a "saving necessity," as Karl Menninger suggested?
- Are you able to say, "I'm willing, but I need help. I want to do what God wants me to do today"?

I'm challenging you to connect to God's spiritual path and become one with God. Stories of transformed alcoholics, redeemed drug addicts, and transformed criminals after meeting God are legion. Yet there are just as many stories of new life brought to cratered families and friendships after an encounter with God. I've been lucky to see many of these transformations in my ministry. When I see a changed life, it reminds me of a song by Don Francisco called "He's Alive." This song tells the story of how God restored Peter after his denial at the enemy's campfire by embracing him following the resurrection. The song says that as Christ embraced Peter, "Guilt in my confusion disappeared in sweet release. And every fear I'd ever had just melted into peace."

When you come to Christ, it will change you forever. He changes you and makes you new. He smooths out the rough edges of your life and brings joy.

So I say there is power and help for your life and relationships. Connecting to God and gaining true spiritual direction for your life will transform you. Because when you come to God, he changes your life. He lifts you up. He makes you *more*.

I think back over my life and realize whatever true joy and success and happiness I've achieved was based on the care that I received from others. It started with my mom and dad. The privileges I received from being part of that stable home environment and being part of a group of people who cared about me were huge. I owe a lot to my parents. I owe an incredible amount to my wife. I owe a huge amount to the teachers who taught me. I owe a tremendous amount to a couple of Boy Scout leaders I had in my life. There are many coaches and athletic directors that have made a difference in my life. And, of course, I owe the ministers of my life. I owe those teachers of God's Word who lifted me up, took me higher, and helped me dream of becoming more than I ever thought I could be.

There is an inspiring song that often plays on Christian radio stations. It has a powerful message for us all. The song, sung by Josh Groban, is called "You Raise Me Up." Who raises you up? The song can remind us of those who help us to become more than we are. It is a tribute to those who inspire us to greatness.

Exercise

Who are some of the positive influences in your life? Who raises you up? Why don't you call or write them today and thank them? For more, see Matthew 5:6, Luke 1:51–53, and John 4:14.

"No enemy is worse than bad advice."
—Sophocles

Note

[1]Karl Menninger, *Whatever Became of Sin?* (New York: Hawthorn Dutton, 1973), 199.

Chapter Seven

POOR COUNSELORS

Be careful who you listen to.

Some of the worst advice I have ever received involved a boy I will call Romeo. I was in ninth grade and we were in gym class playing dodgeball, when I hit Romeo with a ball, putting him out of the game. This really upset him. He made an obscene gesture at me and that, of course, upset me. We exchanged angry words, and that should have been the end of it. Unfortunately, the next class on our school schedule was homeroom, and both of us were in the same class. Some of my buddies came up to me and said, "You shouldn't let him get away with that insult. You need to show him who's boss. Go over there and punch him. You need to show him that he can't get away with doing that to you." To me, they were extremely wise ninth graders. I assumed they were more experienced at life than I was. So, I went over to Romeo and hit him on the side of the head.

Regrettably for me, none of my friends mentioned that he had been studying karate for years. I ended up walking with a limp for the next three days and being expelled from school. That was when I started learning to question the wisdom of my counselors. Without a doubt, the encouragement to hit Romeo was some of the worst advice I've ever received. To my dismay, I've had other advice given me through the years that turned out just as badly.

One hidden danger of a healthy relationship involves where you get advice. Who do you seek counsel from when you are in trouble? Who do you listen to when you have relational challenges? In previous chapters, we discussed that in a lot of relationships, it's easy to know where the problems come from. It is easy to spot the danger of infidelity to our families. We can see the danger of addiction. The damage done by betraying our mate is easy to comprehend. But some things are not as obvious. One of the hidden dangers that I've seen bring trouble to people's lives is listening to poor counsel. Sometimes when people get into a challenging situation—their marriage is in trouble, their kids are having problems, they've got a business situation that is out of control, or they have fallen into spiritual distress—they simply listen to the wrong people. They act on poor counsel, and it makes their problems even worse.

Who do you listen to when you get into trouble? Be especially careful when someone says, "God told me to tell you something. . . ." When it comes to listening to God, make sure you are getting his directions *firsthand*. If God wants to talk to you, why wouldn't he tell you himself?

Are you having trouble in your relationships? Maybe your marriage is struggling, or you're having trouble with friends. Perhaps there are difficulties in your relationship with your children. You don't know what to do. So you decide to get some advice and cash in on the wisdom and experience of others. In fact, the Bible instructs you to do just exactly that. Several times in the book of Proverbs, we are told to seek good counsel.

- "The way of a fool is right in his own eyes, but he who heeds counsel is wise" (Prov. 12:15).
- "Without counsel, plans go awry, but in the multitude of counselors they are established" (Prov. 15:22).
- "Listen to counsel and receive instruction, that you may be wise in your latter days" (Prov. 19:20).
- "Plans are established by counsel; by wise counsel wage war" (Prov. 20:18).

In other words, the Lone Ranger mentality for solving all your problems is probably not the best way to go. It is wise to seek out the wisdom and experience of others. Yet even more important than getting counsel is making sure you get *good counsel*. It is crucial to make sure the people you listen to can be trusted and that they are capable of giving good advice.

Let me share with you some stories from the Bible about receiving bad advice. The first is the story found in 1 Kings 13 about a prophet of God who was deceived by a false prophet. The prophet was lied to by someone he should have been able to trust, and the result was real tragedy in his life, ending with his death. It is hard to believe that one prophet would lie to another, but that is exactly what happened. Perhaps God was testing his prophet. We may question why God would let him die since he was essentially tricked. After all, he was only responding to the information someone else gave him, and God seems to judge him very harshly. But one of the truths of the spiritual life is this: the more you are given from God, the more God requires of you. Maybe God was saying, "I've shown you enough of myself that you ought to have enough sense not to believe a guy is speaking for me just because he claims to do so."

How do you get the advice you need in life? I once looked at an Internet website that listed celebrities talking about the best advice they had ever received. People listed all kinds of things. Some of the things listed on the site were what you'd expect. People listed common things like, "Make a good first impression." Another celebrity said the best advice he ever received was to read everything. He was challenged by the advice: "Readers are leaders." Comedian Eddie Murphy once said, "People will always be quick to give you advice. Just remember *you* are at the controls." A lot of people can identify the best advice they have received in life, but what about the worst advice? Looking back at your life, can you see some areas where you got poor advice that made a situation worse?

Let's look at another biblical example of the damage caused by receiving poor counsel. 1 Kings 12 records a story of some of the absolute worst advice ever given in history. The story goes that when King Solomon died, Rehoboam his son took over the throne. However, because the kingdom under David's rule one generation before had been through a civil war, some of the tribes weren't sure whether they wanted to follow King Rehoboam. They got the leaders of the twelve tribes together to meet with Rehoboam. They said, "Look, your father was pretty harsh on us. He demanded high taxes from us. If you could give us just a little breathing room financially and back off the taxes a little bit, we will be your loyal subjects."

Rehoboam was a young man, so he asked his wise older counselors who had served his father what to do. They said, "What the tribes are suggesting is a good plan. You start easy, cut back on these guys' taxes a little bit, and show them you've got a heart. You can work with them a little bit and they'll follow you forever."

Unfortunately for Rehoboam, he then talked to the young men he hung out with. He asked his pals, "What do you think I ought to do?" They said, "You need to tell them their plan is ridiculous. You should tell them, '"And now, whereas my father put a heavy yoke on you, I will add to your yoke; my father chastised you with whips, but I will chastise you with scourges!"' (or *scorpions*, in the KJV) (1 Kings 12:11). In other words, show them who's boss. Get tough. Don't be a wimp. Let them know you're a powerful king. Go out there and say, "I'm in charge. You'd better back off, or I'm really going to lay it on you."

I hate to say this, but young people rarely give good advice. It's not because they're not smart. It's because they're not wise. And you know how to gain wisdom? You get wisdom through experience. You have to live through enough experiences to acquire real wisdom. Rehoboam made a huge mistake. He was influenced by his peers and said, "That sounds good to me."

- Can you think of a time when you sought advice and it turned out badly?
- What could you have done to ensure you got good advice?
- Did you seek advice from a wise source?

When he came in and told the leaders of the tribes he was going to be harsh instead of lenient, the kingdom split in two. Instead of being the king over twelve tribes, he was left with only two, and the nation plunged into civil war. He had received terrible advice, really terrible advice, and unfortunately for him and for Israel, he acted on it. Don't make the same mistake as Rehoboam. Here are three things you can do to protect yourself from poor counselors.

Examine your methods for choosing counselors. Sometimes when we're in trouble, the hunger that we have to share the pain of our lives or seek to understand it can lead us to talk to people who are not trustworthy. When we are hurting, we want to share our heartache. When we are in pain, we want people to know we are suffering. When our hearts are broken, we so desperately want consolation that we often talk to those who are *not* trustworthy. Let me give you some advice that comes from years of counseling people in crisis. When you get into a situation of heartache and emotional pain, talk to *as few people as possible.* Don't tell everybody about your personal problems.

When I do premarital counseling, I instruct couples that when they have a fight, they should keep the fight between just the two of them. I warn them not to share it with everybody. It is natural when in conflict to want to build a coalition, but *don't do it.* What often happens to a couple is they get in a fight, and then they call parents and friends and tell them all about the disagreement. They describe how horrible their mate is and the terrible things they did, and they get consolation and support. Then the mate comes home with flowers and an apology, and suddenly they are in love again. Now they are happy with their mate, but their parents and friends have taken sides and want to fight the battle.

So do not share with people out of your pain unless you are sure they're completely trustworthy. The rawness of the pain you feel may lead you to be careless with personal information. In order to protect yourself from bad counsel, first examine your methods for choosing your counselors.

- Who checks your thinking for wisdom when you're in trouble?
- Who do you turn to for advice when you have relationship issues?
- Are your counselors worthy of wise counsel? Do they have experience?

Examine the motives of your counselors. We need to remember that not *every* counselor has our best interests in mind.

People sometimes tell us things with ulterior motives. The entertainment industry is infamous for giving out poor advice in order to make a dollar. We are being deluged with information through radio, television, computers, and personal devices (not to mention Twitter and Facebook and the like) and not all of it is good.

Have you ever made a decision about something because of a song you heard on the radio? Perhaps you were going through some kind of situation, and you were thinking, "Oh man, I don't know whether to leave or stay. I don't know whether to fight or love. I don't know what to do." And then you heard a song on the radio, and you said, "That's it! Yeah, that's it, that's the perfect solution!"

Perhaps you should stop and think about the song you just heard. Why did they write that song played on the radio? Not for you. Not for your problems. Not for your difficulty. Not for your pain. Not all music gives sound advice. They wrote that song to make money. They don't care about you; in fact, they don't even know you. You need to be careful what you listen to.

Have you ever made a decision based on a movie? I must admit I have. One decision came from the movie *Rocky*. The movie was about a prize fighter, and there were some extremely moving scenes showing the hero getting into shape for a big prize fight. If you saw the movie, you'll remember that Rocky drank raw eggs. He put eggs in a glass and drank them down, and then he went for a run. I was so moved by that movie with its dramatic music and powerful visuals that I got some eggs, broke them into a glass, and drank them. Then I went for a run. I made it about a quarter of a mile, and those raw eggs were on the sidewalk. They were awful! That was a nasty thing to do. I could have gotten salmonella poisoning doing that. It was crazy to make a decision based on a scene from a motion picture. Movies, songs, and novels are a great source of entertainment, and they are not necessarily bad. But they are entertainment-based, and you need to examine the motives of the people giving you information in those formats.

There are people who will listen to your problems and give you advice, but these people don't always want what's best for you. People giving you advice about your relationship may not care about your relationship at all. They might be jealous of your happiness. They might not even like you. Be careful who you listen to. Make sure they want what is best for you.

Examine the success of your counselors in the field for which they are offering advice. If you're going to take advice from someone, doesn't it make sense to check his success rate? Why would you accept somebody's advice if she's not successful in the area in which you're asking? Would you ask a mechanic how to fix your car whose own car is always broken down on the side of the road? You wouldn't ask a landscaper how to fertilize your yard if his yard is patchy and full of weeds. That's just common sense. If you are asking people for relationship advice, you ought to look at the success of their relationships. When you seek out a pastor for pastoral advice, see how healthy the church is that he pastors. If you are asking people for advice to deal with your children, watch how they interact with their own children.

There is an instructive story in the Bible about poor counsel found in 2 Samuel 13. It is a terrible story of deception and deceit that leads to violence and death. The Bible tells about a young man named Amnon who was one of King David's sons. Amnon had become infatuated with his half sister, Tamar. He was very distressed over his sister because she was a virgin, and it was obviously improper for him to pursue her.

Amnon had a friend, Jonadab, who was the son of Shimeah, David's brother. The Bible describes Jonadab as a very crafty man. He notices Amnon's sadness and learns that his friend is lusting after his own sister. What should he have said to Amnon? He should have hit him on the side of the head and said, "Get over it! That's your sister." But he was crafty, and instead he created an ugly plan to enable Amnon to take advantage of this young girl. He counsels him to pretend to be ill and request that Tamar come feed him. Jonadab tells him that his father will not refuse this wish because of his feigned sickness.

Amnon does as his friend suggests, and when his sister comes to cook for him, he sends his servants out of the room and rapes her. We don't know if Jonadab told Amnon to attack his sister or not, but he did give him a deceitful plan for getting his sister alone with him. This brutal attack set off a series of events that would lead to Amnon's murder and eventually to civil war in the kingdom. A young girl was defiled, a kingdom was thrown into conflict, and thousands of men died. All of this pain came about because Jonadab encouraged deception.

He was a crafty man. When he was asked for advice, it wasn't straightforward, honest, spiritually wholesome, godly advice that he offered. It was a plan to be slick and tricky. There are always people who've got slick plans. There are always those who come up with a real tricky way of handling challenges. If somebody's giving you information that sounds something like "Hey, you know, here's a tricky way to do this," run away. Be wary of people giving you advice that encourages deception. The best counselors are often those who have the courage who tell you no. In your financial life, you need a CPA who will look at you and say no when you ask him about a questionable monetary move. "No, you can't do that. That's a bad thing to do." You need a doctor who doesn't just tell you what you want to hear, but tells you what's good for you. You need a physician who pushes you away from the spareribs and toward the bran cereal or at the very least counsels moderation in your consumption. You need a counselor for your emotional health who tells you no at times.

Sadly, when it comes to advice, some people will just keep asking until they find someone who will tell them what they want to hear. They ask about an unwise move in their relationships, and when their advisor warns not to go forward, they ignore that person and move on to another counselor. Then they just keep asking until they find someone who agrees with their idea. Sometimes it is good for us to hear negative things, especially if the same rebuke keeps coming. If just one person tells you that you look like a donkey, you can ignore him. And if two people tell you that you look like a donkey, you can kind of shrug it off. But if four or five people tell you that you resemble a donkey, maybe you ought to start looking at saddles.

Wouldn't we all be wise to listen sometimes when we're getting negative advice?

- Have you ever refused advice because it wasn't what you wanted to hear?
- Have you ever followed advice that was tricky or sly?

The most serious place to seek counsel is in our relationship with God. We need to learn how to walk with God and improve our interactions with others. The Bible tells us a story in the third chapter of the book of Genesis about a counselor who encourages cynicism toward God. You know the story. God has created Adam and Eve, and they live in the luxurious Garden of Eden. Everything is wonderful. They are blessed by God's presence every day when he comes to walk with them. They enjoy perfect health and have absolutely no stress. It is literally heaven on earth.

Then, in chapter three, the serpent shows up and encourages them to doubt God's love. He insinuates that God only wants to hold them back in life by denying them knowledge, when they, he says, can become gods themselves. He encourages Adam and Eve to break the one commandment God has asked them to obey. After hearing the serpent's advice, they do just exactly what he tells them and eat the forbidden fruit. You know the rest of the story. This disobedience gets them kicked out of the garden, and they become mortal for the first time in their existence. As a result of their disobedience, the world is plunged into sin. The perfect environment of the garden is no longer available to them. Now they must live by the sweat of their brow. Every pain, disaster, and heartache that has happened in the entire history of the world started with that one sin.

That one sin started with cynical advice. The serpent asked, "Did God really say that?" He implied that they didn't need to take God seriously. Sometimes we get in situations and we say, "You know, I'm kind of thinking I'd like to have this or that in my life of pleasure, or I'd like to enter into a new relationship," and the Bible says no. You talk to a friend about your conflict with God, and they say, "You know, you don't need to take the Bible that seriously." The question becomes, "Did God *really* mean it when he forbade the things we want to do?" We begin to doubt God's clarity, and then we start turning away from God's wisdom. That usually means heartache and pain in our relationships is on the way. Listen, God doesn't stutter. If he said something is forbidden—*he means it!* The Bible describes the Ten Commandments, not the Ten Suggestions. It's always easy to get into trouble when we listen to a counselor who gives us cynical guidance. So be especially careful of those who give cynical advice about God.

Let me share a paraphrase from a powerful verse from the Bible: "My dear friends, don't believe everything you hear. Carefully weigh and examine what people tell you. Not everyone who talks about God comes from God" (1 John 4:1 *The Message*). The sad truth is that there are some preachers in this world who lie. Not everybody who tells you "God said" knows what they're talking about. And some who do tell you that God speaks to them only want to merchandise your life. You want to know where to get advice spiritually? Why not follow the advice of Jesus? He told us in the Gospel of Matthew how to tell the good preachers from the bad preachers.

Jesus taught:

> Beware of false prophets, who come to you in sheep's clothing, but inwardly they are ravenous wolves. You will know them by their fruits. Do men gather grapes from thornbushes or figs from thistles? Even so, every good tree bears good fruit, but a bad tree bears bad fruit. A good tree cannot bear bad fruit, nor can a bad tree bear good fruit. Every tree that does not bear good fruit is cut down and thrown into the fire. Therefore by their fruits you will know them." (Matt. 7:15–20)

Check the fruit on the tree! Good preachers and teachers produce good results. Their advice helps people get better in dealing with the struggles of their lives. Look at the people around the good teachers, and you will see they are healthy people. Their families are healthy. Their lives are good, wholesome, honest, and decent. Before you go seeking spiritual advice from ministers, ask yourself, "Do they have healthy lifestyles, healthy families, and healthy followers?" Check the fruit on the tree because your soul could depend on it. There are people who just want to get in your pocketbook and just want to build a crowd. They don't care if your family is destroyed by their advice. They don't care if their teachings make you miserable.

All they want is a crowd to listen to them and money to fill the plates.

Be careful. Look at the fruit. Use discretion. Use wisdom. Don't let the danger of poor counselors add to the pain in your life.

Exercise

Create a checklist to post on your computer or write in a notebook of guidelines to follow for good counselors. Make the first question to check on the list whether or not you have sought God's advice before that of any friend or advisor. For more, see John 3:18–21, 2 Timothy 4:3, and Job 21:14.

"If you are car shopping, never look at the Ferraris first."
—Unknown

Chapter Eight

THE COMPARISON PARASITE

Learn to value your loved ones for who they are, not how they stack up against others.

One of my personal heroes is Ralph McCoy, ThD. He was a veteran missionary of fifty plus years. He started his missionary career in the country of Costa Rica back in the 1940s. After several years of success, he became very ill and almost died, but he managed to make it home to the United States. Eventually, he transferred to the mission field of Mexico and served God there for many successful years. I got to know him personally in 1968. He was home for furlough and had developed an extremely debilitating medical condition. Dr. McCoy was dangerously thin and could not gain weight no matter how he much he ate.

One of the effects of his illness was a muscle problem that pulled his head to the side. The only way he could look straight was to hold his head in place with his hands. After many batteries of medical tests, doctors finally concluded that while in the jungles of Costa Rica, he had contracted a parasite. A microscopic organism took residence in his body. It grew and multiplied until it was literally threatening his life. Thankfully, the doctors discovered this tiny enemy and were able to cure him and save his life. All of his symptoms dissipated. He was completely healed.

The interesting thing is, it took years to realize that he was in danger. That's the thing about parasites. They slip into our lives without our noticing them. They're small and unobtrusive. They take up residence and begin to feed off of us. Eventually, they begin to do real damage and steal life from us. But parasites do not only exist in the physical realm—they also exist in relationships.

We all know the dangers of addiction. We all know the dangers of infidelity. We all know the dangers of gambling and other obvious perils. But there are other dangers that can slip in and ruin our relationships. We need to be aware of these unobtrusive dangers that can result in divorce and alienation. These dangers can produce heartbreaking separations between friends and family, parents and children, and husbands and wives.

One of these pitfalls is the bad habit of comparing ourselves to others. I call it the parasite of comparison. This relational parasite can bring great destruction to our emotional lives. This includes looking at others and judging ourselves in accordance with them, or even allowing someone to judge us in relation to others.

What does this relational parasite of comparison look like? It can be a husband who compares his wife's beauty and attractiveness to other women. This is a very destructive thing. Men typically don't realize that when they express their admiration of other women, they can cause a lot of pain to their spouse or girlfriend. The parasite can also be a wife who compares her husband's business or career success to that of other men. She may say things like, "Why aren't you more successful?" Or she may say things like, "Why aren't you doing more?" "Why can't you be like my friend's husband?"

The damage can also come from parents who compare their children's academic or sports abilities with those of other children. Perhaps they make statements to their child like, "I'm disappointed in you. How come you don't do as well as Johnny or Susie?" The emotional impact can be particularly negative when a parent compares one of their children's abilities with that of another sibling. I can say with gratitude that I never heard such statements from my parents: "Why aren't you like your brother?" "Why aren't you like your sisters?" However, I did hear a version of this kind of comparison from my school teachers. I was blessed with an older brother who was handsome, talented, popular—he was a golden boy. So all through school when I would move up to a new grade level and meet new teachers, they'd say something like, "Oh, you're Donnie Beckham's little brother!" I got so tired of being referred to as his "little brother" that I started answering: "No, I'm Kim Beckham. Donnie Beckham is my older brother."

Comparison can be a painful thing. When young people are compared to each other, wounds form easily because they are still establishing their self-esteem. Teenagers constantly gauge themselves against other adolescents. They ponder: "How do they look? Do I look as good?" "Am I as smart or as popular as she is?" You could say someone whose mind creates a constant mental comparison to others has "keeping up with the Joneses" syndrome.

For people who get stuck in the comparison mode, every day is like pop quiz day at school. Didn't you hate pop quiz day? You go to school and everything's going fine until the teacher says, "Pop quiz!" Then you start to sweat because you immediately wonder if you are ready. When you spend your days in comparison mode, that's how life feels. We pepper our minds with questions:

- "Why am I not as thin as she is?"
- "Am I going to do alright?"
- "Why are my kids not more like theirs?"
- "How do my clothes compare with everyone else's?"
- "Why can't my wife be more like Jim's wife?"

When you live in comparison mode, life will never be enjoyable. This is an easy trap to fall in to because we live in a society that is driven by comparison. Advertisers manipulate us with comparison. The before and after pictures that are constantly used in advertisements force us to mentally assess our looks and possessions against those of others. Mass media gives us false and deceptive images to emulate.

This is particularly painful for women and girls in our society because they are presented with unrealistic (and often unhealthy) images of feminine beauty. The images of beautiful women in our society are often complete distortions. I love to see those television shows where they grab celebrities and stick a camera in their faces when they least expect to have their picture taken. Man, do these supermodels and movie stars look different! In such candid tabloid shots, they look startlingly normal. But when you see them on a magazine cover or on a television show, they look drastically different! Why? The lighting is manipulated, the makeup is professionally applied, the hair is styled perfectly, they've physically prepared for months with a personal trainer, and the film crew shoots at just the perfect angle to highlight their beauty. Of course they look fantastic! Yet people compare themselves to those staged pictures of pampered stars and say, "Boy, why can't I be like them?" Many may feel ugly in comparison to such stars when the reality is: it is all an illusion! Those celebrities don't even look like their staged and airbrushed pictures. Still, many people compare themselves to others because of the mass media.

Competition, which drives our economy, is also ripe with comparison. Sometimes this can be healthy. Competition helps keep us on our toes, but sometimes too much can endanger our relationships. Even in the realm of physical fitness, comparison can sneak in and distort our experiences. Fitness ought to be about getting healthy and strong. Unfortunately, it's often corrupted into endless mirror gazing as people compare their bodies to others in the gym. When you go to the gym, it is important to acknowledge how you look and the areas that need work. And at times, you certainly need to assess progress toward your fitness goals. But the purpose of working out is to feel healthier and improve physical strength, not to compare your own progress with others.

- Can you think of an area in your life where you have been comparing yourself with others?
- Do you have memories of being unfavorably compared with siblings or other children?
- Does someone close to you verbally criticize herself because she doesn't look like others?

Even in the realm of faith, comparison can be a problem. Church success often becomes more about who has the biggest crowds instead of who is helping people connect with God.

Turn in your Bible to 2 Corinthians 10:12. Though slightly out of context, it does have to do with comparing ourselves and our spiritual gifts. Sometimes, there are people in the church who can't enjoy being children of God because they're not as good at teaching, preaching, singing, or praying as somebody else in the congregation. In 2 Corinthians, the Apostle Paul is fighting for his right to be recognized as an apostle, and he accuses people in the church of attacking him. He said of these people, "For we dare not class ourselves or compare ourselves with those who commend themselves. But they, measuring themselves by themselves, and comparing themselves among themselves, are not wise."

He said these people were criticizing him and saying things like, "I'm a better teacher than you." "I have more experience than you." "I can read more Greek than you." "I've been around Peter longer than you." Paul expressed that this is ridiculous! Spiritual maturity is not about who has more skill or who is the most talented in some area. This type of maturity is about how close *you* are walking with God. Indeed, spiritual comparison is a very destructive thing.

So exactly how does the comparison parasite attack our healthy relationships? One way it does so is to create dissatisfaction with ourselves and make us unhappy. Many people are not happy with themselves. They think of themselves as failures. They feel they ought to be better or more successful. These people never say, "God, thank you for making me exactly who I am." Instead, they look around at others and make comparisons. In their frustration, they say things like, "I don't have as much as others do," or "I don't have a big house like those people do," or "I'm not like them," and they make themselves miserable. Even worse, one trait of unhappy people is that they believe they ought to share their misery.

I was at a car dealership one day getting some work done on my car. The waiting room was crowded with people, and there was one man there who was loudly complaining about what a rotten day he was having. He kept going on and on about his car troubles and how much they were an inconvenience. I wanted to pull him aside and remind him that everyone in the room was there for difficulties with their vehicles. Nevertheless, he was not content until everyone else was just as miserable as he was.

Another way comparison attacks healthy relationships is to fill our minds with myths and lies. Comparison is often inaccurate and unfair. It's the "grass is greener" syndrome, right? Humans are always looking over the metaphorical fences of their lives and saying, "Boy, that sure looks better over there." We wish our wives could be like some other women we have met. We wish our husbands could be like other men we know. We wish our kids could be like the seemingly perfect children of other parents. People are always looking over the fences of their lives and daydreaming about someone else's seemingly perfect life. But be careful what you wish for.

As one down-home philosopher said, "The grass might be greener on the other side of the fence, but you've still got to mow it." This myth of comparison only works because we mostly see people when they are at their best. We see them in public after they are well-dressed and groomed and on their best behavior. We often don't *really* see them and what happens in their home behind closed doors. We don't see them unless they are totally put together.

It's like the difference between your driver's license and a professional photograph. Take a moment to get your driver's license out of your wallet and look at the photo. Then compare it to one of your family photos that has been professionally photographed. It's obvious which one is the most flattering, isn't it? This is the problem with getting caught up in admiring those with lives that seem more perfect than ours. We see the staged shots of their lives, the posed and scripted images they create for the public. But we are not *really* seeing them at all.

There are obviously some things about them that would not be so appealing if we were to spend a month in their home. So beware the comparison trap of the "greener grass" syndrome. Remember that comparison is often inaccurate and unfair because it's a surface and limited judgment.

Comparison to others can also become a trap for our pride. Sometimes people compare themselves at the expense of others to boost a lack of self-esteem. We can slip into feeling superior to our friends or our mate because we are feeding our pride. There's a great passage in the Bible about spiritual pride that illustrates this point. Jesus' parable is found in chapter 18 of the Gospel of Luke. Here's how it goes: two men went to the temple to pray. One of them was a religious leader in the community. This religious leader, a Pharisee (for that was the title of their religious party), looked around, and beside him in the worship service was another man the Bible calls a publican. A publican was a tax collector for the army of Rome which, at the time, was occupying the nation of Israel. Such were often associated with bribery and extortion, and most people considered them terrible sinners. The Pharisee stood and prayed out loud: "God, I thank You that I'm not like other men: extortioners, unjust, adulterers, or even as this tax collector. I fast twice a week; I give tithes of all that I possess."

The story continues,

> And the tax collector, standing afar off, would not so much as raise his eyes to heaven, but beat his breast, saying, "God, be merciful to me a sinner! I tell you, this man went down to his house justified rather

> than the other; for everyone who exalts himself will be humbled, and he who humbles himself will be exalted. (Luke 18:11–14)

This is a classic example of pumping up our pride by comparing ourselves to people who make us look good. Have you ever done that? You think to yourself that since you're not feeling too good today, you're going to pick on somebody. Let me share a story.

One day, I was in my church office chatting with a couple of our staff members. We were laughing and joking together. Our children's pastor has a twelve-year-old son who was a part of our group that afternoon. I was feeling pretty good about myself because I had been working out at the gym with a personal trainer. So I challenged this twelve-year-old boy to an arm-wrestling contest. Now, the important part of this story is who I did *not* challenge to wrestle. My associate pastor was there and is in very good physical condition, but I didn't challenge him. My children's pastor was also standing there, and I didn't challenge him, either. I challenged a twelve-year-old boy I outweighed by over a hundred pounds. Why did I challenge him? Because I knew I could easily defeat him, and that is exactly what I did. I was just goofing around with him that day, but the point is this: Wouldn't it be silly for me to be proud of beating a child in arm wrestling who is one-fourth of my size?

We create a dangerous type of pride when we start comparing ourselves to others, especially if we seek out easy targets to make us feel better about ourselves. This is exactly what the Pharisee was doing in this passage of the Bible when he proudly thought to himself—I'm glad I'm not like that wicked tax collector.

The issue should never be: How do I stack up against other people? The issue should be about how close I have come to reaching my full potential. It's my potential that is the gauge of progress. The question should never be whether or not I'm more spiritual than another person. The question is: Am I as spiritual as *God* wants me to be? The gauge of my career success is not how I compare to another colleague, but am I as successful as I *could be* given my innate gifts and talents? How I measure up against my full potential is the real question. Refusing to compare myself to others can keep me from slipping into the trap of pride.

Another reason comparison is bad for us is that it discounts our uniqueness and refuses to recognize the distinctiveness of others in our lives. We are all uniquely made, and comparison robs us of the pleasure of enjoying our diversity. It also denies individuals the freedom to be who they were created to be. For instance, a child who's a math genius may be made to feel inadequate because she's not a sports star. Instead of looking to or at other people and comparing ourselves to them, we should focus on the uniqueness of God's design for our lives.

Let me give you an example of the fallacy of comparison thinking. Artists create all different kinds of art. In my office, I have a few different pieces of art. I have a wood sculpture called "Prayer" from Malaysia. The statue is of a Malay islander, and he's bowed in the attitude of prayer. I love this statue. I also have some paintings on the wall of different subjects and scenes. Some of the art in my office is large, and there are several large canvas paintings. However, some of the pieces are quite small. For instance, I have a piece that someone brought me from the Crazy Horse Reservation in South Dakota. It's a stamp of the great Indian Chief Crazy Horse that's been etched in fine metals. It's intricate and small, but beautiful. The point is, some of the art in my office is large and expressive, while some of the art is intricate and small. Now, can you imagine the artist who created the intricate and small art looking at it and saying, "I don't like you. You're not large and expressive"? That would be utter nonsense! If you asked him about the size of his work, he would probably say, "I created it to be unique. I wanted it to look just exactly like it does. I designed it to be small and intricate. I don't compare it to the big paintings on the wall because I created it to look like it does on purpose."

We have a Creator God who created each one of us. The powerful truth is: he created each of us to be exactly who we are. When we look at another person and say, "I wish God had made me tall instead of short," or "I wish God had made me petite instead of tall," we are insulting our Creator. God would say to us, "This kind of thinking is ridiculous! I made you to be you. I delight in exactly who you are." Why do we feel we all have to look alike anyway?

When it comes to our physical appearance, I believe people are more like sandwiches than they are like muffins. Have you ever made muffins? If you have, then you know that you make the batter and then you pour it into a pan that has little molds in it. After they are finished baking and you take them out of the oven, they all look pretty much alike. But sandwiches are much more unique—especially if you get to make them yourself. Maybe you have your own special sandwich that you make with a specific assortment of meats, cheeses, and condiments and then you stack them just so. As people God created, we are more like sandwiches than muffins. God doesn't put us in a pan and flip us out looking identical to everyone else. The fact is he *wants* us to look different. He delights in our distinctiveness because it's a reflection of his creativity. When we compare ourselves to other people, and we compare our loved ones to others, we are robbing them of their uniqueness and individuality.

Another trap of the comparison parasite is that it can cause us to feel aggrieved toward God for the way our lives are turning out. We may feel that he doesn't treat us as well or bless us as much as he seems to bless others. I have seen church members become disappointed in God because they are envious of another believer who seems to have a better job or a better family. They begin to question God and wonder why they don't have as good a job or as healthy a family as someone they know—the implication being that God has been unfair to them. We fall into this type of comparison trap when we resent others who don't have the challenges and struggles we face.

Perhaps you have had a severe illness and you wonder why others are well. Maybe you lost your job and others seem to be prospering in their work. The comparison bug leads you to ask the question, "Why am I suffering and others are not?" That's a difficult question and there could be many different answers.

There is a parable found in the Bible that addresses this kind of dissatisfaction. You will find the story in Matthew 20. Let me summarize this passage for you. Jesus was talking strongly to the Jewish people and explained: "Look, you're upset because I have come and reached out to non-Jews. And you've been saying, 'Hey, wait a minute. We've been followers of Abraham for centuries, and now all of a sudden you're coming and saying that God is going to bless the Gentiles in these last times." So he told them a story. He said that a farmer had a field, and he needed to get his crop in. So he went out early in the morning to the marketplace, got a bunch of workers, and said to them, "Hey, do you want to go to work in my field today? If you go, I'll pay you a penny." They said, "We'll take the job." They went to the field and started working. Halfway through the morning, he needed more workers. So he went and hired more workers with the promise of a penny for their work. They agreed and immediately went to work in the fields. He repeated that action several times during the day, and when the day was almost done, he realized he still needed more help. He went back again to the marketplace, talked to some more men, and said, "I'll pay you a penny to go to work in my field for the rest of the day." They agreed and headed for the field even though the day was nearly done.

At the end of the day, as he was paying all the workers their money, the guys who got there at 7:00 A.M. saw him giving the same amount of money to the guys who arrived to work at 4:00

P.M., and they said, "That's not fair! That's not fair! You're giving them the same amount of money as you are giving us!" They were comparing themselves to the other workers, and they felt they were being mistreated. Jesus said the farmer responded to their complaint by saying, "Wait a minute. Friend of mine, I'm doing you no wrong. Did you not agree with me for a penny? Take what is yours and go your way. I wish to give to this last man the same as to you. Is it not lawful for me to do what I wish with my own things? Or is your eye evil because I am good? So the last will be first and the first last, for many are called but few are chosen" (Matt. 20:1–16, my paraphrase).

The point of this story is that God says, "It's my field, and I'll do what I want with what is mine." The application to us is that if you're God's child, don't complain of challenges in your life that you think others do not have to face. And don't gripe that you are not getting what other people are getting from God, because you belong to him, and he is entitled to do what he wants with his own property. When we are discouraged by some of the challenges God allows us to go through, we can find comfort in remembering that God values everyone who belongs to him and his ultimate plan is always for our benefit. We need to remember that God's field is his to do with as he wills, because he knows how to make it the most productive and valuable it can be.

The Old Testament prophet Jeremiah said it this way: "'O house of Israel, can I not do with you as this potter?' says the LORD. 'Look, as the clay *is* in the potter's hand, so *are* you in My hand, O house of Israel!'" (Jer. 18:6). God is saying: "I'm the potter. I will do what I want with the clay in my hands. If I want to make a bowl out of this, then I'll make a bowl. If I want to make a jug to hold wine, I'll make a jug. If I want to tear up the whole piece and throw it away, I'll do that. You don't get to tell me what to do with what is mine."

This is the clear teaching of the Bible about submitting to God's control in our lives. We are not to second-guess God and complain about his work in our lives, and yet we do it all the time. We moan, groan, complain, and gripe because we don't have the same possessions that others have. We whine to God that he is not being fair. And God says, "I own you through Christ, and you have committed to following me. If I have this unique purpose for your life, then I can do with you as I wish." For some people, this creates an aggravation. Maybe you are aggravated with God. You're just mad at him. You don't like what God has allowed in your life.

Perhaps you question why God allowed a tragedy to occur in your family. "Why did God let this happen to me?" you ask in the dark hours of the night. I can understand that pain. There are things in my life that I really wish he hadn't let happen to me. I don't know why God allowed me that pain, and I don't know why God has allowed your challenges. What I'm saying is: God has a right to do what he wants with those who are his. Faith means that we trust God to always have our best interests in mind, even if we don't understand the current circumstances of our lives. Faith means that we see ourselves as God's possession, and we don't compare our lives with other believers.

Faith means that we trust God to do whatever he wants with our lives.

- When you compare yourself with others, do you become mad at God for what you see?
- Have you ever challenged someone weaker than you in an attempt to make yourself look better?
- Do you compare your children, husband, or wife to others? Do you secretly judge them?

What are some cures for the comparison parasite? The first cure is to accept the value that God, your Creator, has placed in you. All of us are beautiful in our own way. We need to remember that each one of us has been specially designed by God to be unique. We must refuse to let comparison attack our self-esteem. It simply doesn't matter how we compare up against others because each human is a treasured creation of God. "God created each of us, and God don't make junk." He simply doesn't.

Second, refuse to grade yourself by other people's standards, and don't let other people grade you either. Never let people tell you that you should do this or you should do that. I don't mean you shouldn't listen to those who challenge your academic grades—and we all have to obey the laws of society. But when someone starts comparing you with someone else, you must reject their assessments. Never tell yourself that you should be this tall, or that weight, or this fast, or that strong, based on someone else's opinion. Also, refuse to wallow in false pride based on an unfair comparison with others. Remember, just because you can beat a little boy in arm wrestling doesn't mean you are strong.

Third, learn to cherish the good characteristics found in your friends or mate and do not focus on what is lacking. I have seen couples make this mistake. One or both spouses will focus on a particular trait they don't like in their partner. Remember: *everyone* has flaws. We can focus on the flaws in our mate, or we can look for the good in them.

There's a great story in the Bible about the first time the followers of Christ were called Christians. It happened in the city of Antioch. After Christ's resurrection, the church exploded in numerical growth. The believers stayed in the city of Jerusalem to start with, and then persecution from the Jewish leaders drove them out. Some of the believers went down to Antioch in Syria, and they began to preach the gospel to whoever would listen. It wasn't long until many of the Greek nationals began to follow Christ. Upon hearing about this movement of God, the church in Jerusalem decided to send several church leaders to check out what was happening. So these orthodox Jews traveled to witness what was going on in Antioch. One of these men was called Barnabas. The Bible says that he was also nicknamed the Son of Encouragement.

When Barnabas went to visit these new Greek followers of Christ in Antioch, he could easily have found a lot of things wrong with how they worshipped Christ. If you compare ancient Greek culture to that of the ancient orthodox Jews, there were many differences. To the Jews in Jerusalem, these Greeks would have appeared to have many flaws. They were brand-new followers of Christ, and Barnabas could have focused on the minor flaws in their worship and lifestyles and judged them harshly. But instead, the Bible says that he commended them for their faith and encouraged them. Then he went home.

I once heard a great pastor preach a sermon on this passage called "Looking for Grace or Grime." His point was that people will find what they are looking for. When you look at loved ones, children, a spouse, friends, or even your pastor—you're going to see flaws. If you look for good, you will find things to admire. So choose to focus on the good.

What should you do when someone you care about doesn't compare favorably with others? Here are a couple of suggestions: first of all, make up your mind to nourish and protect that relationship. Your attitude should be, "I don't care if we are having a problem. I don't care if I'm struggling. I am going to protect and nourish this relationship." Secondly, identify and appreciate his or her strengths. Focus on what you love about that person.

Another suggestion is to, when it is possible, expose your friend to helpful resources. I hesitate to share this idea because you could mess it up, big time! You're going to buy a weight loss program for your girlfriend and get in a lot of trouble! Don't do that! But when it's appropriate, and in a very tactful way, suggest opportunities for improvement.

Here's a good idea—practice being an example of the change you desire to see in others. If your mate is having trouble with his spirituality and is not praying or practicing spiritual disciplines, why not ask, "Would you like to join me for morning prayers? Would you like to attend Bible study with me?" One final means of dealing with a poor comparison you are making with someone is to publicly affirm your friend or mate—simply brag about them. Nothing will make you appreciate your mate, your friend, your church, or your pastor more than bragging about them. Make it a practice to tell others how wonderful they are. You will find that people will agree with you in a hurry as you praise your friend, and when they do, you will be affirmed in your opinion. Realizing that others can see the good in your mate that you see will cause your appreciation of that person to grow.

Recently, a dear friend of mine underwent open-heart surgery. This friend is someone that I have counted on for over twenty years. As I waited prayerfully for his surgery to be over, I contemplated how much he meant to me. I would have been devastated if his procedure had not been successful; thankfully, it turned out very well. What I realized is that I *need* the people in my life. As I sat there in that crowded hospital waiting room, any minor annoyances I might have had with my friend disappeared. I just prayed my friend would be okay.

If God would bring him back strong and healthy, I wouldn't mind his flaws as much. Deep inside, I realized that this is how I felt about all my friends and family. None of them are perfect (as I surely am not perfect), but it is still a blessing to have them in my life. Right there, I made the decision not to allow the parasite of comparison to contaminate one more minute of my relationships with the people who make my life a joy. I hope you'll make the same decision. Becoming aware that a person you care about might be taken away forever puts the relationship in perspective and the comparison habit disappears.

Perhaps you are judging someone in your life right now; you're constantly comparing someone you love with others. But when you realize that if the person were to be taken from you—what a hole it would leave in your life—the need to compare them with others goes away. You might have a parasite of comparison that's chewing on you and ripping up your personal relationships at this time in your life. Constant rating and judging might be poisoning your relationships with your children, your mate, your friends, and your church. Perhaps what was once a tiny thought of criticism in the back of your mind toward someone you love has grown and is working against your relationship.

Allowing yourself to think people you love don't stack up like they should, or don't look like you think they should, has become an ugly habit for you. The little parasite of comparison is breeding toxic waste into that relationship. If you don't get a grip on such a negative mental habit, *it will ruin* relationships. Determine today to stamp out these ugly bugs. Refuse to participate in the habit of comparison. Instead, make an effort to fall in love again with the uniqueness of your friends, mate, and children. Get rid of the parasite of comparison. Life is a lot better when we debug it.

Exercise

Obtain a live bug, caterpillar, or a june bug. Keep it in a sealed container this week and take it everywhere you go. Each time you look at the bug, let it remind you how the parasite of comparison can hide in your mind and poison relationships.

"We must all suffer one of two things: the pain of discipline or the pain of regret or disappointment."
—Jim Rohn

Chapter Nine

LACK OF DISCIPLINE

Any relationship worth having
is going to take work.

One of my favorite books is called *Eat That Frog*, by Brian Tracy. In fact, I like the title even better than the book. The concept of the book is, theoretically, that if you had to eat a live frog every day, the best course of action would be to eat that frog first thing in the morning. After doing that, everything else in your day would be pretty easy by comparison. I have to agree with this logic. This helpful book addresses dealing with procrastination. It's about dealing with those things that we tend to put off for one reason or another. Unfortunately, many of us have a tendency to procrastinate. Actually, I've even procrastinated reading books on procrastination!

I recently saw a top ten list on the Internet of why people procrastinate.[1] Maybe one of these will resonate with you:

10. Keeps you very un-busy
9. Make other people crazy
8. Too lazy to flip a coin
7. Get the ice cream later
6. I was gonna clean . . .
5. Even thinkin' about doin' somethin' hurts
4. Early bird?
3. A good reason
2. Dancin'
1. Procrastinate, and someone else will do it!

Whatever their reasons, people seem to love to put off what they don't have to do right at that moment. People drag their feet doing everything from going to the doctor, to paying their bills, to cleaning the garage, to purchasing a burial plot—even dealing with the profound spiritual issues of life. They also take their time dealing with interpersonal conflicts and other relational issues.

Lacking the discipline to deal with problems in our relationships is definitely a hidden danger that can damage those relationships. While some relationship dangers are very easy to spot, sometimes we don't see other serious hidden time bombs until it's too late. We let our relationships drift or don't pay attention to them. People put off the required maintenance to keep those relationships strong. Then they are surprised when the relationship crumbles into wreckage, and they are emotionally devastated. The average person doesn't like to face facts: good relationships require work; they don't just happen by accident. Good marriages don't just happen. Successful parent-child relationships don't just happen. Lifelong friendships don't just happen. They all take work and work requires discipline. That's why lack of discipline is a serious hidden danger to any healthy relationship.

First, let me define what I mean by *discipline*, because when you look the word up in the dictionary, there are several definitions. One meaning for discipline is when you have chosen a particular area of growth to work on, such as a discipline of study. Of the definitions listed in the dictionary, perhaps the most familiar have to do with the area of punishment: "punishment designed to teach obedience." Another definition is the ability to behave in a controlled and calm manner, even when you are caught in a difficult or stressful situation. This is the essence of a disciplined personality.

This ability to display a conscious control of one's lifestyle is the discipline I want to discuss in this chapter. It is self-control used for directing or changing behavior. (The use of discipline to learn something or to train for something is what I'm referring to.) Everyone has the mental capacity to control his or her behavior.

We do not have to be the pawn of circumstance in a relationship. We do not have to be blown about by the random conditions of our lives. There is a way to display discipline in our emotions and in our relationships. How? Decide what you want out of your relationships rather than simply accepting good relationships as a matter of luck and good fortune. Self-discipline is a conscious decision of how you are going to live life. It means taking conscious control of your lifestyle.

One truth of life is: the harder we are on ourselves, the easier life gets for us. For instance, if you set up a personal financial budget and live under the discipline of scheduled spending, you will have an easier life. There is no doubt that it's a lot less painful to restrict your spending than it is to have creditors calling your house and hounding you for late payments. The harder you are on yourself, the easier life gets for you. Apply this truth to your educational experience. If a student starts a term paper weeks before it's due, rather than waiting until ten hours before the deadline, he or she will write a better term paper. In his great book *The Road Less Traveled*, M. Scott Peck said of discipline, "It's the basic set of tools required to solve life's problems. Without discipline we can solve nothing. With only some discipline we can solve only some problems. But with total discipline we can solve all problems."[2] I don't know if we can solve all problems, but I know that we can make significant improvement in our lives if each person practices self-discipline. Let's examine this issue of taking conscious control over your life and your thinking.

- What does a life of discipline look like as far as relationships are concerned?
- What area of your life currently lacks discipline?
- Why do you think this area is out of control?

What does discipline look like as far as how you deal with your children, your spouse, or your friends? It might be easier to start by looking at the opposite to stir our thinking. So, what does a *lack* of mental discipline look like in relationships? Here are ten examples. Maybe one will sound familiar.

Verbal volcanoes. People suffering this lack of discipline immediately say any thoughts that come into their minds. Some people may even be proud of this trait. However, having a filter between the brain and mouth is a good thing. Don't you agree? Have you ever realized that you said something out loud when you believed you were just thinking it? "Did I say that?" you wonder. That mental filter is there to protect you. It simply is not wise to verbalize *every* thought that comes through your head.

For example, have you ever wished you could read other people's minds? Don't wish for that because you really don't want to know. Wives are always asking me, "What is my husband thinking?" I say, "Ladies, you really don't want to know what he's thinking." First of all, I can assure you as a man, most of the time he's not thinking anything. He's really not!

Verbal eruptions are a classic form of poor discipline. When some people are angry and frustrated, they just let their frustration spew out and dump hurtful words on whoever is around. Later they may regret them, and they may even apologize for their outbursts. However, it still doesn't take away the sting of the verbal lashing out. We need to avoid being verbal volcanoes.

Excessive daydreaming. What are the symptoms of excessive daydreaming? Fantasizing about immoral scenarios. Or wasting time visualizing the perfect friend, child, parent, or spouse. Some people have a negative imagination at work in their minds all the time. They're always comparing their mate or their friends to some fantasy of a "perfect" person. They spend long amounts of time fantasizing, "Oh, if I only had that person as my husband," or "If I only had this situation in my family, then I'd be happy." There's a big difference between setting goals for what you want and negative daydreaming. So be wary of the type of daydreaming that focuses on negative comparisons of the people you love with people or ideals from your fantasies. Excessive daydreaming can do real damage to relationships.

- What is in your "emotional garage"?
- When was the last time you cleaned your emotional garage?
- Is it affecting or hindering other areas of your life?

Emotional laziness. Negatively expressed, it can be that there are some areas that need to be dealt with, and we simply don't. It's like the household chore of cleaning the garage. The great thing about having a garage is that you can put lots of stuff in it. The bad thing about having a garage is that there's a lot of stuff piled up in it. Does this sound familiar? Sometimes it gets to the point that the only thing you can do is put the door down. Finally, the garage gets so crowded that you can't even get your vehicles inside anymore because you've got all that junk piled up. You say to yourself, "I'm going to clean the garage today," but for some reason you don't do it. Then you say, "I'm going to clean the garage next week," but again you don't tackle the chore. This pattern can continue for years . . . even decades!

It's the same way in our emotional lives; we have areas of communication that have been neglected. Emotional laziness can take the form of an unexpressed or unspoken expression of love and support. It can be failing to spend time on important relationships. We make the mistake of letting other things get in the way of dealing with important relationship issues.

There's a bittersweet moment for families at every high school graduation. Parents find they are both proud and sad at the same time. It's exciting because their child is accomplishing a great milestone in life, but they're also sad because they realize a stage of life is ending. The opportunity that they had to bond with their loved one before he or she becomes an adult is slipping away.

Why do we wait until people are gone to think about sharing what they mean to us and how much we care about them? Don't let emotional laziness rob your relationships by failing to take advantage of those precious opportunities. Don't fall victim to emotional laziness.

Pampering bad habits. Some people have harmful emotional habits that they protect by defining them as personality quirks. For instance, they may say something like, "Well, yes. I know I'm sometimes too angry or self-centered," or "I know I don't say the things I ought to say to my kids, but that's just who I am." If you have been following a similar pattern, face the fact that "just who you are" is hurting other people and you need to change. "Just who I am" is a lame excuse. Everyone is born who he or she is, but where will we be if we resign to stay who we are and fail to mature?

Every week at church, I pass by the toddlers' class. Sometimes I stop to observe the little children running around in their room and enjoy watching their energy and innocence for a few moments. Yet I don't wish those little saints would stay just like that forever. I won't reveal which parent's child it was, but one day when I went by for a few minutes, this little darling was putting Oreos in his ears. That's amusing behavior for a toddler, but it would be a pretty embarrassing thing to do when you are turning nineteen. "Just who I am" is a terrible excuse. If who you are now is damaging and hurting other people, be an adult and change immediately.

Emotional hiding. We hide our feelings from the important people in our lives. If you've ever had someone say to you, "I never knew you felt that way," you may be guilty of hiding. Discipline is doing the thing that needs doing whether you feel like it or not. There are times when we are upset with our mate about something. We are not merely annoyed but really feeling angry. Instead of bringing the issue out into the open with a caring discussion, we hide our feelings—not out of fear, but out of laziness. We don't want to expend the time or energy on what might be a difficult conversation, so we hide it away in our heart. This is a lack of discipline.

Lying to others or—worse—lying to yourself. Do you lie about the real issues of your heart? One of the best questions I've ever heard is, "What are you pretending not to know?" There are times we indulge in self-destructive behaviors and try hard to ignore our nagging conscience. "What are you pretending not to know about the way you spend your money? Do you have a negative habit of spending every dime you make instead of laying aside at least a portion of your income for savings? You might be pretending not to know that someday your car will break down or your child will get sick and you'll need some extra money. Refuse to allow a lack of discipline to let you lie to yourself and others.

Grudge holding. We have been looking at some areas of emotional damage caused by lack of discipline. Holding a grudge is a common one. I believe that holding a grudge is a matter of emotional laziness, because it takes *real work* to forgive others. Let's face it, forgiveness is not easy. It can take a strong exertion of will to forgive those who hurt us, but it pays big dividends in our emotional lives when we work to apply ourselves in this crucial area.

- What is the longest someone you know has held a grudge? Days, weeks, years?
- What was the disturbance over? Was it something big or small?
- Was it worth it?

Denial. You may refuse to acknowledge a problem out of stubbornness or fear. Others may easily see the difficulties that are cropping up in your emotional life, but you just keep insisting that it is not a problem. Let me give you an example. My automobile came equipped with a verbal warning system to help me operate it more safely. It has a voice that instructs, "Please buckle your seat belt," if I begin driving without buckling the belt. Most of the time I appreciate that helpful voice, but there are times when it annoys me. In fact, there have been times when I was tempted to get out my owner's manual and search for a way to turn that voice command off. It would be a foolish thing to do (as far as safety goes), but sometimes I just don't want to hear the reminder.

We can do the same thing in our emotional lives. People can shift into denial mode when their hearts are crying out for attention and trying to warn them that they are headed for an emotional crash. To ignore these warnings is to display a true lack of discipline and is a dangerous thing to do. Still, I see this *all the time*. Something unpleasant or something difficult comes up in some people's relationships, and what do they do? They run away! That's denial.

Caving. I am not talking about spelunking into holes in the side of a mountain. What I mean is that you cave to emotional pressure when you ought to be standing firm. People cave because they put the need to be liked above the need for healthy change.

This behavior is easy to see in parenting. The reality is, it can be difficult to be a parent at times—especially if you want your little angels to like you, like I did. I wanted my daughters to love me, and thankfully, they did. Occasionally, I'd have to discipline them in some small way and often they would start crying, and as their dad it would break my heart. They would cry those big crocodile tears and ask me not to ground them or restrict their activities, and instead of being ready to punish, I would be instantly ready to cave. This is why God gave me my wife, because she would rescue me. After a discussion about discipline, they'd run to their rooms crying. I would be crushed as I listened to them weep. I'd say to my wife, "Barbara, they're in there crying!"

Barbara is a wise woman and understood which tears were serious and which were not, and she always said, "They'll get over it." And they always did. In situations like this, parents want to cave because we want our children to like us. Yet a parent's job is not to be a buddy or friend to their child. Their job is to be a guide, a director, a developer of character. Sometimes that means children are not going to like their parents. It means they're mad at you for a while. Remember, they'll get over it.

Friendships can be a place we allow ourselves to cave out of lack of discipline. Perhaps in one of your relationships you have a friend who continues to treat you with disrespect. The behaviors are small but annoying, and they are mounting up. You make up your mind that you are going to stop spending time with them. Then you get a phone call that asks why you are avoiding them and instead of telling the truth, you cave into the pressure of having them like you and you make up excuses and dodge the issue. Your lack of discipline in doing the hard thing makes it very likely that you will continue to be taken for granted in the future.

Procrastination. This area is different than denial in that you admit you have a problem, but you just keep putting off dealing with it. I once saw a T-shirt that said, "Top 10 Reasons People Procrastinate. Number One"—and then the rest of the shirt was blank. Think about it. Don't put off dealing with problems. Show some discipline and get moving on difficulties as quickly as you can.

Did any of these reasons seem familiar?

How can you get started improving your self-discipline? The first concept to understand is that discipline begins in your thoughts. You must discipline your mind before you discipline your behavior. We must force our minds to think through our actions in advance. We must think through the possible consequences of our actions before doing something. This is the effective use of mental discipline. Robert Ringer, the bestselling author of *How You Can Find Happiness During the Collapse of Western Civilization*, calls this practice "future-oriented thinking." He has written that the most successful people in the area of personal discipline are the people who can mentally project the consequences of their decisions out into the future. In other words, the farther out in the future you can think about your behavior and how it will impact your life, the more likely you are to be self-disciplined.[3]

People are much more likely to set aside money on a weekly basis for retirement if they can clearly visualize forty years from now what their situation will be like. Future-oriented thinking is a powerful key to self-discipline because the reality is that all of our actions have consequences, and all our behaviors will produce a response. We must force our minds to think through the possible ramifications of proposed actions.

When contemplating a new course of action, ask yourself, "What is the potential result of this attitude or behavior?" And when you ask yourself that question, look honestly at all the answers that come to mind. If you want to change your life, here's a powerful question if you can bring yourself to bravely answer it: "What am I *pretending* not to know?" Sometimes when we choose a behavior or we choose an attitude, we do so and pretend not to know better. Ignorance is not bliss; ignorance is destructive, and people who have good relationships don't play games with the truth in their lives. Don't ever be guilty of knowing that deep down something is a bad decision, and move ahead because you don't want to deal with it. That's a big mistake. It's huge!

- When was the last time you had a feeling of "I know better than this"?
- Do you remember what the situation was?
- How did you react to those feelings?

Let me remind you of a story from the Bible. It's an ugly story, and we have already looked at it once in this book, but there are some powerful truths contained in it. King David had several children. Of course, being a king in ancient Israel, he had multiple wives. Therefore many of his children were half-brothers and half-sisters. David had a son named Amnon who fell in love—more honestly, fell in lust—with his half-sister Tamar.

He wanted her and devised a plan whereby he could rape her. When she came out of that horrible situation, she ran into another brother, Absalom, and she told him what had happened. King David was made aware of this crime, but he took absolutely no action to punish Amnon. Absalom hated Amnon because he had raped his sister, and his hatred was undoubtedly intensified by his father's inaction. David got angry—but that's all. He didn't punish Amnon. He did nothing. What an example of pretending not to know something unpleasant.

What were the results of David's lack of discipline? Tamar was neglected, her chances for marriage were ruined, and she was shuttled to the side of the kingdom. Absalom grew to hate his brother and lost respect for his father. Absalom eventually murdered his own brother in revenge for his sister's rape. Then Absalom tried to overthrow his father's reign, plunging the entire country into civil war out of lack of respect for David.

What if David had said to himself, as soon as he was made aware of Amnon's crime, "If I don't take action to address what happened here, what are the potential consequences?" What if he had taken action? Tremendous misery could have been averted and his family might have been salvaged. David paid a high price for his blissful ignorance. Let me ask you a question: What are you pretending not to know, and what is the potential damage that can be caused by your refusal to face reality?

Honestly, facing the demons of our inner lives is difficult and scary. Psychologist Scott Peck talks about the challenge of psychotherapy where people examine their inner lives. He says that entering into psychotherapy is an act of great courage.

Laying ourselves open to the challenge of honestly probing the hidden areas of our lives is daunting. Most of us would rather not look into the dark cellar of our thoughts. It's scary in there.

As a pastor, I've been called on to do marriage counseling and am always nervous about working with church members on their marriages. Often, I share with the couples I counsel that it may affect how comfortable they feel attending our church. In order to solve the problems in their marriages, they will have to tell me the dark secrets of their marital lives. That's fine with me. It won't bother me to know their secrets. God has given me a pastor's heart that always sees the good in people, but it's possible that it will be hard on them when they're sitting in the pews on Sunday morning and knowing that I know what happens behind closed doors.

A few families have actually left the church after counseling because they couldn't bear to be known that intimately. Yet we must not use the fear of being known as an excuse for not dealing with our problems. There are no good excuses for not digging into the areas where you have problems. Perhaps you can look back over your life and see that you might have avoided some emotional wreckage if you had taken courageous action to face a problem instead of trying to dodge it.

- In what area of your life have you been pretending there is no problem?
- Make a list of the positive and negative consequences of your behavior.
- What actions would help you deal with this issue?

The New Testament book of Colossians gives some wonderful spiritual advice about changing our lives that makes a good model for dealing with our emotional baggage. In chapter three, we read about these things that we're to put to death in our lives; the Bible uses the term to "put off" these things, and there is a list of things we're to "put on." Let's look at those briefly, and then I want you to do something.

> But now you yourselves are to put off all these: anger, wrath, malice, blasphemy, filthy language out of your mouth. Do not lie to one another. . . . Put on tender mercies, kindness, humility, meekness, longsuffering; bearing with one another, and forgiving one another. . . . But above all these things put on love, which is the bond of perfection. (Col. 3:8–14)

It's a great list, isn't it? Kill off the bad and therefore put it to death. A different translation uses the words "cut off the bad." Kill off sexual promiscuity, impurity, lust, doing whatever you feel like whenever you feel like it, and grabbing whatever attracts your fancy. Those are the big sins that affect our outer life. Paul didn't stay with just the big stuff though. He went on to address the inner life. He admonished his readers to put off or cut off bad temper, irritability, meanness, profanity, and dirty talk, and to stop lying to one another. These are all inner issues. These are all emotional challenges. Controlling these behaviors is a means of connecting with people.

Instead, the apostle encourages us to put some things on. Dress yourself in these positive characteristics: tender mercies, kindness, humility, meekness, longsuffering, bearing with one another, and forgiving one another. And, most of all, put on love, which is the bond of perfection. We ought to be busy in our lives about putting this good stuff on and constantly working to get rid of the bad stuff. Put on the good stuff. By the way, genuine love is volitional rather than emotional. Do you know what that means? It means you choose it. Genuine love is something you choose to do. It's not just a feeling you stumble upon.

This is a truth that every happily married couple understands. From time to time, you have to *decide* to love your mate, whether you feel like it or not. No matter how deeply in love you are, there are going to be times when your mate is going to be less than attractive. Even the best partner will at times display selfishness or at least indifference to their partner's feelings. When that happens, the person who genuinely loves their mate does so because of the decision they made to love. Real, genuine love is a choice, not a feeling.

Let me close this chapter with a practical strategy for developing strength in your emotional life and getting more emotional discipline. Remember the list in Colossians of traits for putting off and putting on? I want you to choose one of those that you need to put off. The list includes bad temper, irritability, meanness, profanity, dirty talk, and lying to one another. Choose one of those, or choose one of the positive traits that we were encouraged to put on. That list started with tender mercies and carried on through kindness, humility, meekness, longsuffering, bearing with someone else, forgiving someone else, and putting on love by choice. Choose one of those to put off or put on.

Change is difficult, but our relationships are worth the price of change. Here's a secret to creating a successful change in your life. Take baby steps. Take small steps toward change. I heard an inspiring story about a woman who made a lot of money from a book with an idea that's so simple, it's unbelievable. She specializes in helping people get motivated to clean their houses. She has developed a system for people who just can't seem to get around to cleaning their homes. I'm not talking about those folks who are not willing to clean like a lot of husbands. I'm talking about people who are struggling with getting the cleaning process started.

One of the strategies she has developed is called the five-minute rule. She encourages people to make the decision when they go into a room that needs cleaning that they are going to work for just five minutes. She counsels her clients, "Tell yourself, you are only going to spend five minutes and then you can quit." I think this is a brilliant strategy. I can see myself contemplating cleaning the bathroom, and I really don't want to clean the bathroom. But I can tell myself, "I'm not going to clean the whole bathroom, I'm just going to spend five minutes here." I can do five minutes with one hand tied behind my back. This successful author explains in her book that you often find once you get started, you don't want to stop. It's hard to say, "I'm going to do this whole big job," but it's not hard to say, "I'll do five minutes." You'd be amazed how much money she made off that idea, not to mention how many houses have finally gotten cleaned.

- Do you have a "room" in your emotional life that needs cleaning?
- If you applied the five-minute rule, what would you do first to clean the junk?

You don't have to limit this principle to just cleaning. It works on making changes in your emotional life as well. Let me challenge you about the material we have been reviewing in this chapter. Instead of trying to tackle every area of emotional laziness we have discussed, why not choose only one to go to work on—just one, but make sure you choose at least one. Choose something in your relationships that you need to put off, or choose one of those we've discussed to put on—just choose one. Which of these do you need to put off: a bad temper, irritability, meanness, profanity, dirty talk, lying?

Choose something that you need to put on if you don't want to choose one to eliminate from your life. What trait do you need to add in your life? Do you need to be more merciful? Do you need to be more kind? Do you need to show more humility? Do you need to cultivate meekness? Do you need to grow your longsuffering? Do you need to forgive someone? Do you need to put on love as a deliberate act of free will?

Pick two to start with, or choose one area where you've been lazy spiritually and you've not had discipline. Look at that long list from earlier in the chapter—verbal volcanoes and all those other weaknesses, and choose one thing you need to put on or take off. Got your choice? Now determine to do something about it, starting today. Don't try to change all your areas of struggle at the same time, just start with one.

I want you to make a commitment right this moment to take action. Tell God you are going to do it. Promise yourself and God that, starting immediately, you are going to stop practicing one of the negative traits: verbal eruptions, excessive daydreaming, emotional laziness, pampering of bad habits, hiding, lying, holding grudges, denying, caving, or procrastinating. Say it out loud, "I am stopping right now!" Declare today, "I'm going to take action!"

Exercise

After making a verbal announcement about which negative traits you are going to address, choose which ones you will put on. What behaviors will you put on in place of those you take off? Which behaviors will you put away? Let a close friend or family member know and help keep you accountable. For more, see Ephesians 4:22, Hebrews 12:1, and Colossians 3:12.

"Learned helplessness is the giving-up reaction, the quitting response that follows from the belief that whatever you do doesn't matter."

—Arnold Schwarzenegger

Notes

[1]"Top Ten Reasons to Procrastinate," last modified February 22, 2007, accessed May 31, 2015, https://westwood.wikispaces.com/VI.+Controlling +Procrastination.

[2]M. Scott Peck, *The Road Less Traveled* (New York: Simon and Schuster, 1978), 16.

[3]Robert Ringer, *How You Can Find Happiness During the Collapse of Western Civilization* (New York: Harper and Row, 1983), 110.

Chapter Ten

ASSUMING IT IS PERMANENT

Assigning labels instead of addressing conflicts is the last stop on the ruined-relationship track.

I've been writing about hidden dangers to healthy relationships. After looking at several areas where we can suffer damage to our personal connections, in this chapter I want to focus on one of the most destructive of all the dangers. This is when we make the mistake of assuming that the problem we are having in the relationship is permanent. Just the mental position of assuming that the problem you're facing is permanent can be strong enough to totally derail that relationship.

There are many definitions of "permanent," but the one applicable here is when something is not expected to change. When we get into a relationship squabble and determine in our minds that the disagreement is a permanent problem, that it's set in stone, that it's never going to change, then the relationship is going to be in trouble.

I read a great book a number of years ago by Leslie B. Flynn called *Great Church Fights*. I actually bought it because of the title. Some book titles are better than the book, but not this one. *Great Church Fights* talked about some of the well-known church squabbles and how those congregations handled them. The truth is there are great fights in all kinds of relationships. There have been a lot of great marital fights. If you are reading this book and have been married for any significant amount of time, you know that marriage can be the arena for some powerful struggles. Perhaps you, like this author, can look back over your marriage and identify some fights that have become legendary in your marital history.

Barbara and I have been married forty-two years, and we've had our share of minor tiffs along the way. We've also had a few monumental disagreements. (I think I lost one hundred percent of them.) Most of our arguments were predictable and common. Sometimes it was even fun to be in the struggle. There was a disagreement over where we were going to spend Christmas each year. There were common arguments over spending money versus the saving of funds for a rainy day. Maybe you can look back and see some of the squabbles that you have had in your marriage, or maybe you're in the middle of a struggle right now. Let me share with you a concept from my counseling training that may be helpful to you. There are four steps for conflict resolution attempted by most people in relationships. These are not necessarily helpful steps and can lead to permanent damage to the relationship. But they are often pursued because they are the only methods known.

1. Attempting to persuade the other person to your point of view.
2. Pragmatics of communication: trying to get the other person to hear what you are saying.
3. Power struggles: one-upmanship or one-downmanship.
4. Defining the problem as a core personality issue in your opponent's character.

The first step is an attempt to persuade. In other words, you say to whoever you are arguing with something like, "I just want to explain why this is the best thing to do." "I want to explain to you why eating mackerel patties is better than eating tuna patties." And you have that discussion. And when this first attempt doesn't produce agreement, then you move on to pragmatics of communication. This second level involves communication issues. The other person simply doesn't seem to hear what you are saying, even though you are face-to-face. You're saying one thing; they're saying something else. You are having a conversation, but you're disagreeing over what you're trying to say.

The third step in conflict resolution is the use of power strategies. Much of television humor found in sitcoms that feature families is based on this step. Some classic television comedies have depicted power strategies to make audiences roar with laughter. Think of Lucy and Ricky Ricardo, Laura and Rob

Petrie, or Edith and Archie Bunker, and you will quickly remember some of their struggles to force the other person to their point of view, often with hilarious results. One of the most successful modern TV sitcoms is *Everybody Loves Raymond*. This television show is filled with examples of classic power struggles. I loved the episode where Raymond came home from a trip, and he left his luggage sitting out on the landing by the staircase rather than putting it away in the closet. His brother came over one day and asked him, "When did you get back from your trip?" Raymond said, "Last week." He said, "Why is your luggage still on the landing?" And Raymond pulled him aside and said, "Because I'm waiting for Debra to move it. She's acting like she doesn't see it, but she sees it, and she needs to put it up." Later, somebody else comes over and talks to his wife and says, "Why is the luggage on the landing?" Debra answers, "Because I'm waiting on that jerk Raymond to move it. It's been there for two weeks."

- Who was the last person you had a power struggle with? What did the struggle involve?
- Did you passively address the issue?
- Did your spouse or child clearly get the message?

Raymond and Debra are having a classic power struggle over who's going to win this issue, and they're really getting into it. Maybe you can identify with this example from the show. In power struggles, we take one of two paths: it's either one-upmanship, "I'm going to win," or it's one-downmanship, "I'm going to spoil your win." One-downmanship is when you go along with the other person on a surface level, with plans to undermine their victory. For example, you say to yourself something like, "Okay, we'll do what you want, but if you think you're going to have any fun, you can just forget it." You lose regardless of which strategy you choose in power struggles because the relationship is weakened.

The last step in this poorly thought out conflict resolution, and the point of this chapter, is when you begin to define the problem as a core personality issue. This is the point of no return for that relationship. Once a problem between people is defined as their "core personality," then it's assumed to be unchangeable, and if the problem is unchangeable, the relationship is doomed. For example, no longer is the problem the fact that "my husband won't let me buy the dress I want." Now it's because "he's just a cheapskate and a miser. He'll never change, so why should I even try to work on it?"

Read that last sentence with care. If you're in a relationship of any kind, you need to get serious about whether you are making this mistake. The most dangerous relationship issues, particularly in marriages, are when there are things that you still care deeply about but no longer fight for. As long as you're fighting about an issue, you think there's hope to resolve it. But when you still care deeply about an issue and you're not talking about it anymore and you're not fighting about it, the relationship is in danger of deterioration. This kind of quietness about a volatile issue is a frightening indication that you have accepted that the problem is permanent.

There is a biblical parable we have looked at before that has a lot to say about changing relationships. So let's look at it again. It is often referred to as the story of the prodigal son (Luke 15:11–32). In this story, a son prematurely demands his inheritance and then travels on his own and wastes it. The heart of this Bible story is the personal transformation of this son and how his family reacts when he returns home after his bad behavior. Now, the wayward son has definitely changed. He has changed some behaviors that seemed to be deeply set. He was wasting his father's money, and he certainly didn't want anything to do with his father and his father's way of living, but he changed—he changed his behavior. He changed his attitude and went home with great humility.

We see in the father's reaction to his youngest son's return that he has changed, too, and he has confidence that his son is not the same boy. How do we know this? Because when the son is on the last bit of his journey home, when he is actually walking up the pathway to his home, the father sees him coming from far in the distance. This tells us that the father was hoping for this son to come home. This dedicated dad has not accepted as a fact that this is a permanent breach in the relationship. He is spending a part of every day actually looking for his son's appearance.

Another sign that the father believes his son has changed is seen when he throws a welcome home party. He immediately reinstates his boy to the status of a son without any limitations. Some parents in the same situation might say, "Well, I would have put him on probation and limited the amount of access he had to the rest of my resources." But the father in our story didn't do that. He restored him to his previous full-son status. Why? Because he believed the relationship had changed. He believed that what his son had done was certainly bad behavior, but it was not a trait of his core personality. His child had made bad decisions in his life, but that boy was not a bad son.

Unfortunately, not everyone in the family was so generous in their assessment of the wayward boy. The parable says that the prodigal son's older brother pitched a fit because the father gave a party for his returning brother. He was really mad about it, so mad that he wouldn't even come to the party. It appears that he was jealous about the depth of his father's care for his little brother. I believe the story also indicates the older brother assumed that his brother did not change. We get an indication that this is his attitude because he tells his father that his brother spent all of his money on harlots.

Now, nothing about harlots was mentioned up to this point in the story. Why is the older brother bringing up prostitution and implying this is where his brother wasted all his money? I think it's because he still assumes the brother is a bad seed. Now, out of these three relationship connections—father and wayward son, father and older brother, older brother and younger son—which of these has the best chance of rebuilding the relationship? It is of course the father and the younger son. The primary reason this is the strongest relationship is that the father has not assumed permanence of his son's behavior. Once you assume permanence in interpersonal conflicts, it's over for any relationship.

So, why are people so quick to assume the permanence of problems in their relationships, when everything in life is subject to change? Nothing stays the same! An old saying that has been used by pastors to comfort people facing difficulties is "And it came to pass" (Matt. 7:28 KJV). A lot of passages start with the phrase "and it came to pass" because nothing comes to stay. *Everything* comes to pass. Nothing is permanent. I know that the phrase as used in Scripture is actually just stating that something new has happened, but the idea contained in this old pastors' quip does bring some people comfort. Because it's one of the realities of life. Everything does change. Nothing ever stays the same, including our relationships. Everything in life is in transition. Linear change is the story of our very existence. We are born in transition and continue to be until death. In fact, we continue to change after we die. Even the planet is in constant transition. Since its creation by God, it has been moving steadily toward its ultimate fate of destruction.

- When was the last time God surprised you and changed a situation that you thought was permanent?
- How did he reverse the situation or change the people involved?

We're in transition. Our planet is in transition. Our environment is in transition. Nations rise and fall. The enemies of America come and go. Isn't it funny that when you read a little bit of history, you discover that the people who used to be sworn enemies of our country have now become our allies?

Nothing in life stays the same. Since this truth is so obvious about weather, environment, politics, and just about all of life, why do we so readily assume that relationship difficulties are permanent? Why do we say things like, "This is just the way my husband is," and "This is just the way my wife is—there's no hope of any change"? Why do we so quickly assume that when there is a problem with our parents, the relationship is over because "that's just the way my parents are"? Why do we assume that though everything else changes, our relationships will never change?

To start with, real change is difficult. This is the simple reason so many people do not change: because it's hard to change. Anyone who has been on a diet understands this concept. It can be very challenging just to lose a few pounds because to do so requires a change in habits and behavior that is difficult. It's hard to change anything that's rooted in our habitual behaviors. John Maxwell, a best-selling leadership writer, wisely states: "Change only happens when one of three situations occur. People hurt enough that they have to, people learn enough that they want to, or people receive enough that they're able to."[1]

This is the creed of Alcoholics Anonymous or Narcotics Anonymous: when you get to the absolute rock bottom, and you get sick and tired of being sick and tired, and nobody's rescuing you anymore, then you will change. People change when they hurt enough that they have to. That's why if you want someone you love to change, but you're enabling them to continue their bad behavior, good luck! Why? Because people change when they hurt enough that they have to. People change when they learn enough that they want to. This is the strategy behind all Bible teaching ministries. If you teach people a better way to do something, you can elicit change. When people learn something, when they learn new strategies for old behaviors, then they *can change.*

People also change when they receive enough that they're able to. This truth explains the power of Christianity to transform lives. When people come to God, they receive power from the Holy Spirit to help change their lives. Once they are living in God's power, people can love someone they formerly hated, forgive someone they were cherishing a grievance against, and work to repair broken relationships. God is now in their lives, and they have received enough to change. We need help because change is difficult, and we assume a problem in our relationship is permanent because it's hard to change.

The second reason we assume relationships will never change is that the long-standing nature of some relationship issues can produce discouragement. When a couple has fought over something with each other over and over again, it gets to the point that they assume it's not ever going to change. I was reading *The True Believer,* which is a book about political revolutions. The author, Eric Hoffer, said that most successful revolutionaries lacked any political leadership experience. He went on to say that the men who started the French Revolution were wholly without political experience. And the same was true of the Russian Bolsheviks, the Nazi party in Germany, and the communist revolutionaries in Red China. The people who started those political movements were absolute amateurs in the realm of politics. They had no experience with how difficult political change could be, and it was to their advantage. They were bold in their thinking and unlimited in their vision.

Experience can be a handicap. This is why it is easier for newlyweds to change problems in their marriages than it is for people who've been married long amounts of time. It's probably easier for parents and young people to change their relationship soon after that person leaves the home than after they've been gone for a long time. It can be an easy emotional position to take when something has been going on for a long time to assume it's permanent. The person in conflict says, "Well, you know I talked about it and I talked about it and they've been this way for ten years and it's not *ever* going to change." That may not be true at all, but it's easy to assume that.

Stubbornness on the part of one of the people in a relationship struggle can lead to loss of heart in trying to solve problems. In order for any struggling relationship to get better, both people have to want to resolve the conflict. If only one of the participants is willing to work on the issues while the other remains in an inflexible position, there is little hope of improvement. This is why some divorces are inevitable. I believe God hates divorce, and I'm not a proponent of easy divorce, but some marriages may be doomed to failure.

Theoretically, could God save *every* marriage? Yes, I believe he could! Yet some marriages have no hope for change and are doomed to failure because both participants must be willing to do the hard work of reconciliation and intimacy-building to restore it. When a marriage has one partner who is absolutely committed to bad behavior and is unwilling to change, it is unlikely that there will be any positive resolution. There is certainly no limit to what God can do, but there is a limit to what people are willing to let him do. This is why stubbornness can lead to believing a problem is permanent in the relationship.

- How many people does it take to ruin a relationship?
- How many people does it take to resolve a relationship?
- Why do you think some couples do not try to save their marriages?

Next, poor communication patterns can also contribute to a fatalistic position of conflicts between people. When we're arguing with others, we don't always argue intelligently. We say defensive things like, "That's just the way I am," or "I don't know why I'm like this." If you're in an argument with someone and you're using that kind of language, stop yourself immediately! When you speak in this manner, what you're actually telling the other person is that you're never going to change. This is not only discouraging to your partner, but it is an overstatement of reality. You *can* change and probably will many times in your life. You may not know why you're doing something that's troubling the relationship, but don't tell people that you're doing it because that's just the way you are.

Do you remember the old cartoon *Popeye*? Remember Popeye and his girlfriend Olive Oyl and the bad guy, Brutus? Popeye had these massive forearms and little bitty biceps. He would sing that he was "Popeye the sailor man, toot, toot!" Remember? Stores used to sell *a lot* of spinach because of Popeye. Do you remember Popeye's favorite saying? "I yam what I yam." Popeye would get in a mess and he would say, "I am what I am." That may be okay for cartoon characters, but it's a destructive and limiting position for real people to take in their relationships.

The fact is we are *all changing* all the time. You are not what you were ten years ago. You do not have to be what you were when you were in high school. You are a human being who is highly capable of change. As long as you are not suffering from a brain injury, your brain can still form new patterns of transmission and grow new neuron pathways, and you can learn new behaviors. *You can change!* Be careful never to communicate that you are just "stuck" in your patterns of behavior.

Having a lack of role models who demonstrate successful relationship change can also lead to a feeling of permanence. A lot of people have simply not seen anyone change something significant in their lives. This is a good reason to surround yourself with successful people to observe healthy relationship growth in action. However, just because you have not seen others change their relationships does not mean change is impossible.

Believing a relationship problem is permanent can also be an excuse to quit a relationship. Some people assume a problem is permanent with their marriage or friendships because they want out. Maybe they just don't like the relationship anymore. They are tired of it, so they conjure up excuses: "Oh, he'll never change; it's always going be like this." If you really want to quit on a relationship, then quit. Just do it! However, at least be honest enough with yourself to admit what you're doing and why. Don't cover your action with the lie that the problem is permanent when it very likely is not. It is better to be honest and tell the truth: "I just don't want to do this anymore." Sometimes we claim a problem is permanent in relationships because the truth is that we want to quit.

The final reason for accepting permanence as a fact about our problems is it lets us hide in the role of victim. Some people enjoy being victims. They don't want to believe they can change. Their thinking goes like this: "This problem is a result of my core personality, and I can't do anything about this, therefore I'm not responsible. I don't have to feel bad. I don't have to take any personal responsibility. This negative relationship may be caused by my bad behavior, but that is just the way I am." People may like to play the victim, but the truth is when we take ownership of our actions—everything in this world changes.

- Do you avoid the hard work of change?
- How is stubbornness contributing to problems in your relationships?
- Do you know someone with Popeye Syndrome: "I yam what I yam"?
- How can you address your relationship struggles to avoid the victim mentality?

We do not have to assume the problem is permanent, even if that makes us feel comfortable. So, how can hope be brought back into a troubled relationship? Let me give you some positive steps to follow.

The first thing to do if you want to bring hope back into a troubled relationship is to change your belief about that situation. Reject the mental position of fatalism and overcome the falsehood of permanence. Remind yourself that the way God wired us actually helps to create our reality. We think, then we form beliefs about our thoughts, then we begin to feel emotions about our beliefs, then we act on our emotions. So the first thing to do is think. Then you believe something. Then you feel something. And then you take action . . .

If your thought about a marital difficulty is "she'll never change," then your belief will become that the problem is *permanent*. You will then feel discouraged about the relationship as a result. Since you are discouraged, you will no longer try to communicate or work on the problems.

Therefore, it is imperative that you change your beliefs. You've got to change your perception about the problem because *perception is reality*. If you believe something to be true, it is true for you, whether it's true for anybody else or not. An example of this principle at work is found in the mundane experience of looking for a parking spot at your local mall. Some people never even bother to go up front to look for the good spots. They just park way out in the far reaches of the lot. Maybe this is because they feel young and healthy, and they'd rather walk and not bother with searching for a good spot.

However, some people are just pessimists and have accepted that there will never be any parking places up front. They have internalized the belief there will never be an up-front parking place for them. So they are not going up there to look. These kinds of fatalists believe such an effort would be a waste of time. I appreciate people like that because it means I get to park up front more often. The reality is there will occasionally be an opening up front—and I'm going to get it! Sadly, if you are someone who believes there's never going to be a place up front for you, then there won't be because you are never going to bother to look for it.

I encountered one of the most powerful examples of changing your beliefs and therefore changing your life when I was preaching a series of extended meetings in Weatherford, Texas. The pastor of the church that sponsored the meeting told me the story of his conversion to Christ. When he was a young man, his parents were God-fearing people who loved the Lord and went to church every Sunday and dragged him along. He didn't want to go. He wanted nothing to do with the things of God. He wanted to party and be wild and have a great time. He did agree to go to a summer youth camp one year, and at that camp God touched his heart, and he became a Christian. The experience totally transformed his life for about three months. Then school started up again.

He was not strong enough to resist the peer pressure of negative friends and drifted back to his former bad behaviors. Once again he refused to attend church services. His parents did all they could to encourage him to live wisely and temperately, but to no avail. His father passed away while he was still in high school, and then it was just his mother and him. She pleaded and begged her son to form a relationship with God and to renew his service to God, but he would rather drink beer all night and chase women. He just kept getting in trouble.

He was constantly in and out of jail over minor scrapes with the law and, in his own words, "just wasting my life." He couldn't keep a job, and, of course, that created many more problems for his life. Every time he would see his mother—he did love his mother and they would talk often—she would plead with him to change his lifestyle. She told him, "Son, you know what's right, you know how you ought to live, you know the Lord loves you. I'm praying for you to get right with God and build a wholesome life. I want to see that happen with my whole heart." But as a young man, this pastor would just put her off and refuse to change.

Five years after he graduated from high school, his mother died. He told me that when he went to the funeral and looked at his mother in the casket, all he could think of were her many prayers for him and the things she'd asked of him. He recalled, "I was standing next to the minister who knew me well and knew the situation of my life. I shook the minister's hand and told him that 'I guess it's time for me to grow up.'" He felt sure the minister was skeptical and thought his commitment to change was only an emotional experience. But it was something much more powerful. It was a change in his self-perception.

He told me he left that funeral service and completely changed his life. He stopped participating in negative behaviors and fully embraced the good. He began to work, to hold a job, and to prosper financially. He got married and became faithful to the church. Eventually, God called him to be a pastor. He told me the difference in his life began on the day when he looked down in that casket and saw himself through his mother's eyes. The key was that he saw what his mother thought he could become—his potential. At that moment, he decided it was time to grow up and become the man his mother envisioned. Thus, he changed his perception of who he was. So when the temptations came after that, his attitude was, "I'm sorry, I can't do that, that's not who I am anymore."

- Do you have any relationships that you have written off or resolved are permanently damaged?
- What can you do to change your attitude about that person or relationship?
- How will you approach the relationship differently with a new attitude and through "new eyes"?

Can you see what a big difference changing his beliefs made in the pastor's life? Why not apply this strategy to a struggle you're having? Change what you believe about the relationship. As long as you believe a conflict or situation is not going to get better, it won't. You've got to change your beliefs and expectations.

Secondly, you must change your approach to the discussion of the issues where you have a conflict. If you continue approaching a struggle in the same way with your partner or friend, then you're going to keep getting the same results. Some of you experiencing conflict will actually have to start talking about it again because you have stopped. You have given up. You may have to change your approach because the discussions usually degenerate into the same old personal attacks.

We can fall into habits of communication that are destructive. We may not mean to create more division or strife, but we have become careless in our discussions and fall back on patterns that are negative. Just as we can fall into a pattern of clichés in our prayer lives, we can turn our talks with loved ones into cliché-filled conversations of sniping and cutting remarks. From time to time in our devotional lives, we have to stop and think about what we're actually saying to God. If we don't, we can just mouth routine words that don't really convey our hearts to our Maker. Doesn't it make sense to stop and examine the arguments we're having with the most important people of our lives to see if we are really saying what we feel? Oftentimes, if you will approach that subject from a different perspective, you'll have better luck.

Learn to change what you say to yourself about the situation. We talk to ourselves all the time, and when we talk to ourselves, we often fall into the habit of saying the wrong things. For instance: we might be having a mental conversation with ourselves and saying things like, "This situation is never going to change. I know it's not going to change." To save our relationships, we need to stop. Grab that thought and change it into something positive. Change what you say to yourself about the issue that is hurting your relationship. Change what you think when you see that person you are in conflict with. If you really want to create a positive relationship change, then change what you think.

Did you ever see somebody that you have had a problem with from across the room and say something like, "Ugh! Is that Tammy over there?" Have you ever done that? Unfortunately, when we look at somebody and we say, "Oh no! I don't want to see them," we have a way of expressing that in our body language and demeanor. You may think they don't know what you're feeling, but often many people in the room *will know*. We give off vibrations in our spirit—energy. Some people are better at reading those vibes than others, but most people do read them (often on a subconscious level).

Remember, if you are thinking about a person negatively while you are trying to resolve a relationship issue, your body will project that negativity. It is imperative that you change what you think when you see that person, and instead mentally tell yourself that today God is going to give you a breakthrough. Today, God is going to help resolve this conflict. If you change how you think about the other person, you have a much greater chance to create real relationship change.

Let me close this chapter with this final piece of advice: change the way you pray about relationship problems. Often, we too easily decide that a problem is permanent in spite of a world in which permanence does not exist. Ultimately, whether or not we succeed or fail in any endeavor or relationship has a great deal to do with our worldview, and our worldview has a lot to do with our God view. In other words, it's what you think about God that determines the outcome. Do you see God as big, or do you see him as small? Do you see God as all-powerful, or do you see him as weak? Do you believe what the Bible says in the Old Testament about God's power? God questions Moses: *Has the LORD's arm been shortened?* (Num. 11:23). He is making the point that God's hand and arm are not so short that he cannot save. When you consider the situation where you're struggling, do you see God as able to resolve it? Or do you see the problem as something too hard for God to handle? You have to change your prayer. Let me give you a great verse to lean on: "But He said, 'The things which are impossible with men are possible with God'" (Luke 18:27).

I love this verse. God reminds us that the things we believe to be impossible in our relationships are possible with God. This verse says the struggle you have labeled your permanent problem relationship is not without hope. This verse explains that the relationship problem you believe is permanent and can't be resolved actually can be. Your problem *can be* resolved—or God's a liar. If nothing's impossible for God, then there is *always* a possibility that any relationship problem can be resolved.

Now, does that mean it *will* be resolved? There are a lot of issues that go into deciding whether or not it will be. But hope is always there, no matter how bad the relationship is, because God can do *anything*. It may not be resolved the way you want. However, can God solve your problem? Yes! Will God solve your problem the way you want it solved? Maybe not, but when we believe God is in control and trust him to resolve it in the way that's best for us, then we please him and we can have peace.

- Think of an impossible situation in your life right now that is not resolved.
- Have you turned the situation over to God? Why do you or do you not trust him to resolve the problem?
- What can you do today in good faith to show God you trust his timing and power?

There's an old prayer that challenges me when I read it. It says, "Lord, don't take away our problems but instead grow us so that we are able to handle our problems." God's not going to take away *all* your problems. He's not always going to give you what you think is the right answer for the problems you may face. Yet we have to remember that he is the sovereign Lord. He knows what's best for us. There is pain in life. There is sorrow, and there is failure. There are some relationship problems where you do everything you can to fix them, and they're still not going to be resolved, but there's still hope in that relationship! What is that hope? That hope is that God *will change you.* That God will grow you. God will make you more than you were because he takes that difficult relationship and uses it to produce good in you.

So, whichever way it goes, whether he gives you the answer you hope for, or if he grows you so that you become a stronger, more peaceful person by resolving your conflict in a different way than you wanted, you still have a resolution to the problem. God has still answered your prayer. Have faith that God can do something in every situation. Don't despair. Don't throw up your hands and surrender to hopelessness. Sometimes our relationships are very difficult and we fear they cannot be salvaged, but too often we quit working on the problem way too soon. We use difficulty as an excuse and walk away. Even if things don't get better the way we want, God can still use it to grow us and deepen our faith.

It is always fun to watch little children when they're just learning to walk. They take about three or four steps and they fall on their little bottoms. It's a good thing they wear those big, padded Pampers. What do we say when they fall? We applaud them! We say, "Yaaay! Good job!" As they sit there, they look at us and maybe they think, "What are you talking about? I just fell on my bottom!" Yet we continue to praise them, "Yaaay! Good job!" We praise them because we want them to get up and try again. They do get up and they do try again, and eventually they learn to walk.

Before you know it, they are running and playing. Children fall a lot when they are learning to walk, but their failures are not permanent. When they fall, they get back up. How many times do they have to fall before they learn to walk? We understand this concept of continued effort in spite of failure when we think of a child learning the difficult skill of walking. Why do we not understand this when it happens in our relationships?

We struggle and fight and fail in our relationships, but then we get back up. We struggle in our marriages and we say things we shouldn't, but we get back up. We keep working on our problems and refuse to accept that any problem is permanent and, eventually, we overcome. Never accept permanence! Remember: God can do *anything*. So just keep getting up!

Remember the famous quote by William Somerset Maugham: "We are not the same persons this year as last; nor are those we love. It is a happy chance if we, changing, continue to love a changed person."[2]

Exercise

Write down the last time you felt a relationship or problem was hopeless or would never change. How did you handle the situation? Write down the last time you gave a problem or hopeless situation to God and tried not to "fix it" yourself. Did he resolve it? How do you feel about that situation now? For more, see Genesis 18:14, Ephesians 1:19, and Jeremiah 32:17.

"Whenever you're in conflict with someone, there is one factor that can make the difference between damaging your relationship and deepening it. That factor is attitude."
—William James

Notes

[1]John Maxwell, "Growth = Change," *Injoy Life Club* volume 5, lesson 3, audio lesson collection, The John Maxwell Company. 1991.

[2]William Somerset Maugham, *The Summing Up* (New York: Double Day, Doran & Company, 1938), 306.

Chapter Eleven

REFUSING TO WORK AT RELATIONSHIPS

Every human being is wired for relationships. Nobody is meant to be alone.

When God created us, he made us "herd creatures"—designed to be in a group. That means we were created for relationships. We're meant to connect with others. In fact, most of us crave it. Yet, in general, many of us stink at sustaining and nurturing relationships. In my thirty years as a minister and getting to know people at the deepest level, I've experienced how hard it is for people to make their relationships work. Why is this? Quite frankly, they're building them on the wrong foundation. Most of us are like doughnuts. We have this beautiful, glazed shell on the outside, but at the center of who we are, there's a big hole. We come into relationships with this emptiness, looking to fill the hole in our souls and get our needs met. Still, we can't build relationships on a hole. We can only build them by *becoming whole*—with our hearts intact and our emotions at ease.

In Proverbs 18:24, the New Living Translation says, "There are 'friends' who destroy each other, but a real friend sticks closer than a brother." Isn't that an interesting way to look at friendship—that it has the power to destroy?

- Have you ever met people who were bad influences on each other?
- What qualities made the relationship dangerous?

Sometimes certain personalities do not mesh well in relationships. There are those who are either incapable of compromise or unwilling to stretch themselves for others, and they will always struggle to build any intimacy with others. There are some who are simply too lazy to do the hard work of building relationships so they are probably better off not entering into marriage or deep friendships. Woe to the child who has a parent whose personality is ultra rigid and authoritarian, because the child will never be able to satisfy the parent, no matter how hard they try. There are also people who deeply desire connections with others although they carry emotional baggage that will make it difficult for them to succeed at intimacy. For example, some people can't be without an intimate relationship. They see themselves as damaged unless they are involved with someone else. If only they could marry the right person, they believe they could be whole. On the other hand, some people believe that if they can just get in the right circle of friends, their career will take off. Instead of taking responsibility for themselves, these people expect others to propel them to success.

Some parents even base their relationship with their children on how their children reflect their own success. Rather than simply loving their children as they are, they use their children to feel better about themselves. At the opposite end of the spectrum, some children never quite cut the apron strings from their parents. They look to them as security blankets and won't try their own wings. Instead of building healthy, whole relationships that grow and grow, these types of people destroy their relationships. Why does this happen? At the center of their souls is a persistent neediness that must be overcome.

Why does neediness endanger relationships? It is . . .

- Self-centered
- Based on rescue
- Deceptive
- All about taking, not giving

At its root, neediness is self-centered. "Me, me, me. No, really, let's talk more about me." Have you ever been with people who can't stop talking about themselves? You try to get a word in there somewhere, but there's no room. Psychologists call this narcissism, a morbid delight in one's own self—*morbid* meaning that too much self-interest is bad for us. It also violates Jesus' golden rule: "Do to others as you would have them do to you" (Luke 6:31 NIV). How can we do good to others when we're totally focused on ourselves?

Jesus taught his twelve disciples to be self-sacrificing, giving themselves for others and for the kingdom. James and John pulled Jesus aside one day and said, in essence, "Listen, Lord, when you get into the kingdom, we want the most preferential seats. We want to sit at your right and left hand." Jesus said, "You haven't understood one thing I've told you. If you want to be great in the kingdom, you need to be a great servant on earth. Forget this me, me, me stuff and start thinking about others" (Mark 10:37–43, my paraphrase). When you are with others, are you truly interested in what they have to say? Or do you tend to focus on what others can do for you?

Neediness is also often based on rescue. Psychologist Nathaniel Branden said in his book, *The Six Pillars of Self-Esteem,* that one of the most helpful truths he discovered was this: "No one is coming." In other words, there's no Superman (or Wonder Woman) coming to rescue us. To get out of our own messes, we have to do the work. "If it is to be, it's up to me." So many people get married so that their spouse will "rescue" them. This is a terrible way to go about relationships, and it never works.

- Do you often dream someone will rescue you from a situation?
- Have you ever dreamed of what *you* can do to rescue yourself from that situation?
- Why do you think you are waiting for someone instead of fixing the problem yourself?

Many people are looking just over the horizon—believing that the next relationship will magically change their lives. At the same time, if the relationship they attract is the wrong one, they can't seem to let go of it. Unfortunately, they don't have enough wholeness to say, "I refuse to be treated like this."

Neediness is being afraid to reveal one's true self because rejection is assumed. Needy people avoid being real. They fear that if they are real, others will realize that the hole is there and they'll be rejected. So they conceal their true selves and are never really honest with others.

"Why am I afraid to tell you who I am?" asked Christian psychologist John Powell, in his book of the same name. The answer: "Because you might not like who I am, and it's all I've got." In other words, if you reject the *real* me, I have nothing else left. Needy people hide their true selves in fear that their true selves will not be received. Yet in this deception and secrecy, they deprive themselves of honest relationships and real communication—and the potential for whole relationships.

Needy relationships fall apart when the other person can no longer give what is needed because it is about taking rather than giving. Let's look at a classic example from the Bible. Jesus fed over five thousand people and did it on two occasions. Then one day, he said, "Listen, you're just following me for free food.

- Do your friends and acquaintances know the *real* you?
- When was the last time you held back who you are from others? Why did you hold back?

If you really want to know me, you need to understand that someday you are going to have to eat *of* me" (John 6:26–27, my paraphrase). What did he mean by that? He was using a metaphor to convey an ultimate truth: I'm going to die and my body and my blood will be the sacrifice for you. You'll need to take my body and my blood as the sacrifice for your sins so that you can have eternal life. The crowd didn't like that. Scripture says, "Many of his disciples went back, and walked no more with him" (John 6:66 KJV). Actually, *thousands* walked away from following Christ. They were just in it for the free bread and fish. When they heard the real theology, they didn't want any part of it. This is a classic biblical example of taking rather than giving.

A hidden danger for any relationship is when one of the people involved is only looking to take and not give. As a pastor, when I marry couples, a part of what I ask is this: "Do you take this man [or woman] to be your lawful wedded wife [or husband], and do you promise to love, honor, and cherish, in sickness and in health?" All of these young couples that stand before me are excited about their beautiful mate and the prospect of a wonderful life, but how will it be twenty-five years from now? What if the beautiful mate gets a debilitating disease or is in a traumatic accident? What if he or she becomes someone who needs to be taken care of? Are you committed enough to keep giving?

A chancellor of a university, after many years of great achievements, quit in his prime to take care of his wife, who had Parkinson's disease. People who knew him said, "You're crazy. You could hire somebody to take care of your wife. You're an important man, and you need to be back on the job." The chancellor said, "No. I made a promise to be there for my wife in sickness and in health." Now that's a giver, not a taker.

- Are you a taker or a giver in your relationships?
- What happens when the giver can no longer give?

So, what do other whole relationships look like? Relaxed instead of restless, content despite the uncertainties of life, not needing the constant attention of the other. We see a need for attention often in needy people. They can't give anybody room; they take room and crowd their friends. The message they convey is, "If you don't call me each time you're doing something, if you don't invite me to every event of your life and you're leaving me out, then I'm traumatized." Whole people can be secure in separations. They don't need to be doted on.

I'm reminded of what happened one year in our congregation when two families joined the church two weeks apart. Several weeks later, one couple said, "We're leaving the church." I asked why they were leaving. They said, "Well, your church isn't friendly. We haven't built any relationships. There are a bunch of cliques here. So, we're going someplace else." And I said, "Well, okay. I'm sorry."

Meanwhile, the other family that joined two weeks after the first family had become totally immersed in the church community—from singing in the choir to participating in the children's ministry. "What's the difference?" I asked. "We have two families here. One is unhappy and the other is not." The difference was that one family wasn't waiting for someone to include them. They saw a place where they could *be* a blessing rather than *get* a blessing. The more they gave, the more they got back.

How do we work toward wholeness?

Here are the four essential steps:

- Wholeness means honesty.
- It continues with courage.
- It demands *real* love.
- Wholeness begins and ends with Jesus.

To get back on the path to wholeness, one must first start by being honest. "There are three things you can't protect yourself from," the saying goes. "Bad people, bad timing, and bad luck." Personally, I don't believe in bad luck, but I do believe in bad timing and bad people. There are bad people in the world, and sometimes we can't avoid them. But if bad people are happening to us over and over, there is definitely room for further reflection.

A man I know has been a pastor for over twenty years. He's pastored ten different churches and, so far, has been forced to leave nine of them. What's his explanation? "They can't take strong preaching." Now, any pastor can end up employed at the wrong church. Yet when you've been ousted by nine churches in a row, I don't know if you can blame it all on "strong preaching." Maybe something else is going on.

Wholeness continues with courage. Unfortunately, most people are more comfortable with their misery than with facing the unknown consequences of talking about their problems. My brother has done a lot of work with people struggling with alcoholism. He told me that people in the groups he has worked with often use the phrase "the elephant in the living room" to speak to the problem of denial. Someone will share a story like this one: "I had an alcoholic father. We had this terrible problem in our family. It was ruining us. But nobody would talk about it. It was as if there were a huge elephant in the living room, stinking up the living room, in the way of everything, destroying all of the furniture. But nobody said, 'Look. There's an elephant!'" A lot of us are like that in life. We have some real problems, but we just pretend they're not there.

Becoming whole also demands *real* love. Real love will leave you dissatisfied with anything less than that. When you *really know love*, you can never be happy again with shallow relationships. It's like comparing real ice cream with the no-sugar-added, nonfat kind. Imitations no longer do it for you. You start to prefer the real thing.

Take a close look at your relationship patterns: Do they last long? Are they fulfilling or do you see a similar pattern of problems? It may take some help to find the real thing. It may, for instance, take some counseling or a prayer vigil or a spiritual mentor to work with you on the journey toward wholeness. But once you feel the difference, you'll find there's no turning back.

Jesus said, "You shall know the truth, and the truth shall make you free" (John 8:32). It's so much easier to get whole with the truth of Jesus. That's what I love about being a believer: discovering wholeness begins and ends with Jesus. The glory of our salvation is that not only is it eternal, but it's relational. In the Gospels, Jesus said, "The Son of Man came eating and drinking, and they say, 'Look, a glutton and a winebibber, a friend of tax collectors and sinners!'" (Matt. 11:19). In fact, they always said that Jesus was too friendly with sinful people. In John 15, Jesus said of himself, "No longer do I call you servants, for a servant does not know what his master is doing; but I have called you friends, for all things that I have heard from My Father I have made known to you" (John 15:15).

Jesus' relationship with us is one of friendship. It's not just doctrinal, it's not just spiritual, it's personal—he's our friend, he's our family. The Apostle Paul declared, "The Spirit Himself bears witness with our spirit that we are children of God, and if children, then heirs—heirs of God and joint heirs with Christ" (Rom. 8:16). That's why we often challenge people who have gotten caught up in the concept of doctrine and the tradition of the church—yet seem to be missing a personal relationship with God. My question is: Do you know Jesus Christ personally? Is he your friend? Why? Because that's what salvation is all about. It gets us seated in the heavens for eternity, yes, but here on earth, God himself moves into our hearts and takes up residence. He becomes the friend who sticks closer than a brother. And because it's an abiding relationship, he fills the holes in our souls.

One of my favorite gospel stories is the one about the man who lived in Gadara and was demon-possessed. He was so torn up by spiritual demons that he lived in the tombs, totally isolated. He ran around naked and cut himself with stones. Jesus came along and cast out the demons. Then the people from the city came and saw this man "sitting and clothed and in his right mind" (Mark 5:15). This applies to all of us. When we become believers, we not only get heavenly rewards, but we get clothed and in our right mind! The holes are filled. The neediness is no more.

When the Apostle Paul wrote about what it was like to be filled with God's Spirit, he offered a list of the gifts people have who are spirit-filled: love, joy, peace, patience, kindness, goodness, faithfulness, gentleness, and self-control (Gal. 5:22–23). When the Holy Spirit lives within us and when we have that relationship with Jesus, our chains are gone. Why? Because we've been given the gift of fulfillment. We don't need to take from people all the time. When people are truly filled with the Spirit, they exhibit all of these gifts and are so different. Wherever they go, they leave a refreshing savor. When they are in a group of people, they add a dimension of love, strength, and power that lifts the whole group higher.

Jane Howard, author of a book called *Families*, said about our relational nature: "Call it a network, call it a tribe, and call it a family. Whatever you call it, whoever you are, you need one."[1] I suggest we add the church to that list. A church is a large extended family. Sadly, we live in an age where Christians are under suspicion, and many have lost confidence in the organized church. The church has had its failings, and much has been made of them. But you cannot change the fact that it is a relational organization.

For Christians, healthy relationships are a gateway to evangelism. People have to get to know us before they'll be willing to hear our experience of why Jesus is everything to us. How incredibly important it is that we get good at building relationships. Much of our ability to share the gospel is based on our relationships. The book of Romans says:

> Now hope does not disappoint, because the love of God has been poured out in our hearts by the Holy Spirit who was given to us. For when we were still without strength, in due time Christ died for the ungodly. For scarcely for a righteous man will one die; yet perhaps for a good man some would even dare to die. But God demonstrates His own love toward us, in that while we were still sinners, Christ died for us. (Rom. 5:5–8)

God's love pours into our hearts. So what should we do with it? We should let it spill out on our families, our friends—even those who don't know him yet. The message is this: quit looking to get filled and, instead, get busy letting the love of God flow through you and spill over to fill others' emptiness. Stop focusing on your needs and start claiming what God has done to fill you. Let what has been poured into you flow out abundantly.

Exercise

Go through your mental Rolodex of all the people in your life. Skim past all of the friends and family you enjoy being with. Skip over the people who make you feel good. Now, envision the face of someone who bugs you, someone who is excessively needy—somebody you avoid. Write down that person's name. In the upcoming week, commit to contacting this person and go out of your way to spend time with or do something for him or her without expecting anything in return. Let the love of God flow from you into his or her life. For more, see Colossians 2:9–10, John 14:12, and Acts 20:35.

Notes

[1]Jane Howard, *Families* (New York: Simon & Schuster, 1978).

Chapter Twelve

THE CORROSIVE STAIN OF GUILT

Rid yourself of guilt that keeps you from connecting with others

Bob and Sue dated for years. They got married right out of college, and it seemed as if everything in their lives was positioned for success. Bob started his career, and Sue had two children in the course of three years and decided to be a stay-at-home mom. They made friends, joined a church, and were living the American dream. Everything was fine for about six years until Bob made a fateful decision.

One night while out of town on business, he felt lonely and went downstairs to the hotel bar for a snack, and while ordering, he met a woman. One thing led to another and they ended up having an affair. That one night of passion became the start of a torrid affair that lasted six months. Bob managed to keep his affair a secret from his wife and friends, and he was the one to finally end the relationship. He threw himself back into his marriage and his home life, and he hoped his wife would never learn of his infidelity. But Bob was about to learn a hard lesson. Sometimes when God really wants to punish people for their sin, he lets them keep it a secret. The affair was over, but his unconfessed infidelity kept him filled with guilt and wounded his self-esteem. The emotional torment of his secret life began to impact Bob's personality.

Slowly, his view on life began to change. He became more cynical. He found it hard to believe people's promises and statements because deep inside he knew he did not keep his *own* word. Bob found that he was increasingly jealous of his wife. Even though Sue had never given him any reason to doubt her faithfulness, he began to do just exactly that. His imagination would spin scenarios of her cheating on him with friends—even complete strangers. This led him to frequently question her fidelity to him, and his accusations of cheating hurt her deeply. Their discussions about cheating typically evolved into huge fights, and their intimacy naturally suffered. Bob found it hard to accept Sue's declarations of love for him because in his heart he knew he had lied to her about his fidelity.

Another area of trouble began when Bob found that he no longer enjoyed attending church. Before, he always loved going to church. The Sunday outing was bonding time for his entire family. Now, it had become a source of drudgery instead of joy. He felt like the preacher knew his dark secret, even though his minister had never said anything to Bob about his personal life. It seemed to Bob like some of the comments the pastor made in his sermons were directed at him, especially those that involved the issue of adultery. He began to stay home while the rest of the family went to church, and this led to the loss of one the most powerful bonds that tied his family together.

One day, after months of arguing and frustration, Sue left him a note on his pillow that explained she had taken the kids and gone to her parents' home. She wrote in the note that she could no longer endure his accusations and constant negativity. She wondered on paper where the man she married had gone and asked him not to call her. As Bob crumpled the note in his fist, a tear ran down his cheek, and he knew exactly what had happened. Unresolved guilt had blindsided him and led to the dissolution of his marriage and family.

This scenario is a fictionalized one, but it is based on years of my experience counseling couples in crisis. It illustrates how the aftereffects of our failures and weaknesses can do as much damage as the offense itself. The Bible tells a powerful story about sin and guilt in the story of King David. This wonderful spiritual king won many victories, and his life was *almost* perfect when he fell into moral failure. The sight of a beautiful woman inflamed his passions, and even though she was married, he seduced her and set out to conceal his sin.

After trying several methods to hide involvement with his now pregnant girlfriend, David used his power as king to arrange the death of her husband. Once his lover was free to marry, he brought her to his house to be his wife and probably thought he had successfully hidden his infidelity. The biblical story goes on to recount that a prophet of God was sent to him to let him know that God had seen his sin and would judge him for it; then, a series of calamities began in his life. During this time, David wrote a beautiful song recorded in Psalm 51 that contains some powerful verses relating to the hidden danger of guilt.

David wrote,

> Purge me with hyssop, and I shall be clean;
> Wash me, and I shall be whiter than snow.
> Make me hear joy and gladness,
> That the bones You have broken may rejoice.
> Hide Your face from my sins,
> And blot out all my iniquities.
> Create in me a clean heart, O God,
> And renew a steadfast spirit within me. (Ps. 51:7–10)

How badly we *all* need a clean heart. The anguish David felt can be sensed when he talked about his guilt and described the pain in his bones that had been crushed by God. Now David had not been literally broken. He had no physical ailments. He was writing metaphorically here about how the weight of his guilt on his spirit was crushing.

King David was not the only person to write about guilt. The Apostle Paul declared when he was making his defense before an angry magistrate, "Herein do I exercise myself, to have always a conscience void to offence toward God, and toward men" (Acts 24:16 KJV). Paul said the goal of his life was to have a clear conscience so he would not have to feel guilt. He sought a conscience void of offense before both God and men or, in other words, a conscience that was blameless.

There's not a right-thinking person who doesn't immediately understand the concept of guilt and how limiting it can be in our lives. Have you ever felt guilty? Do you have any guilt issues in your life? Have you stopped to think about how guilt might be eating away at your healthy relationships?

Let me be totally honest—there are a lot of things I feel guilty about. I will share with you my list. As you read through this compilation, you may recognize some areas that ring true for you. First of all, I feel guilty about my parenting. It could have been better. I feel guilty about not being a better husband, not being a better son, not being a better brother, not being more politically correct, and not being more "green"—and I'm not referring to money. I feel guilty for drinking too little water and too much soda. I feel guilty for not being a better Christian and not being a better pastor. I should have been a better boss and leader, and I feel guilty for liking junk food *so much*. I feel guilty about the time I spent playing video games, and I feel guilty for being so bad at video games I played.

I feel guilty for reading mystery novels instead of serious books. I feel guilty at times for pretending I'm really interested in serious books that I'm being forced to read. I feel guilty for all the pastoral exaggerations of my life. I feel guilty for walking on the grass in spite of signs that say don't walk on the grass. I feel guilty for driving in parking lots and pretending not to see that someone else wanted the parking spot I just pulled into. I feel guilty for not working out at the gym more often. I feel guilty for not reading, not praying, not witnessing, not serving, not worshipping more . . . and the list goes on. Do you identify with all this pseudo-guilt? And then I feel guilty because I feel guilty *too much*. And sometimes I feel guilty because I don't feel guilty *enough*! Guilt, guilt, guilt! You get the point, right?

- What makes you feel guilty?
- Have you been trained to focus on rules and expectations of others?
- What *should* you feel guilty about that you *don't*?

Now, I wouldn't worry about guilt issues if we were just talking about the light psychological trauma we experience when we disappoint other people. But there is a more serious issue here. The power of guilt can destroy lives. There's real power connected to guilt. The comedian Woody Allen once said, "When we played softball, I'd steal second base, feel guilty and go back." Some of you know that level of guilt. I'm writing about the serious levels of guilt that bring real trauma to our lives. I am writing about the kind of guilt that limits and defeats us, the kind of guilt that alienates us from others—and, even worse, from God. And the sad thing is we've already been freed from the power of guilt. If you know Christ, it is an exercise in futility to maintain guilt over sins committed that have been forgiven by Christ. Yet a lot of Christians walk around doing just exactly that—feeling guilty.

Let's think a bit about how guilt operates. First of all, it's universal. There are many different cultures in this world, and reasons for feeling guilt can vary from culture to culture. But there is not a single culture in this world that does not know the pain of guilt. Every human on the planet feels guilt. It's universal.

Guilt can also have a huge impact on our lives. We have tremendous psychological issues that spring from guilt. Much of the great literature of the world revolves around the power of guilt to disrupt and destroy someone's peace of mind. Do you remember reading "The Tell-Tale Heart" by Edgar Allan Poe? You remember that? The story was about a man who committed murder, and then he kept hearing the sound of a heart beating in his conscience until it drove him to confess his crime. Remember *Crime and Punishment* by Fyodor Dostoevsky? He wrote of a man who committed a murder, and the guilt of the deed eventually destroyed the rest of his life. *Macbeth,* William Shakespeare's great play, was a tragedy about guilt. Or how about Charles Dickens's *A Christmas Carol*? Three ghosts from his Christmases past caused the miserly Scrooge to feel guilty over being so tight-fisted with his wealth.

Much of the great literature around the world focuses on guilt because *we all* feel guilty, and it limits our lives. Guilt is the hidden danger that wreaks havoc in the courtroom of our self-esteem. It attacks the sense of self-worth that we need to venture out in life. The sad reality is: there's plenty of guilt to go around, and unresolved guilt results in ruination.

But one of the gifts of anger is that it can move us to change, and that's really the basis of guilt and why God allows us to feel this emotion. This is why God gave us a conscience. Phrases that talk about emotional guilt are not common in the New Testament, but the idea of having a clear conscience before God and other people is certainly there.

The Bible teaches that the reason God gave humans emotional guilt is to drive us toward positive change. The purpose of guilt in my life and the purpose of guilt in your life, from God's point of view, is to make you feel angry at yourself when you do not follow God's will and honor him, to make you feel frustrated at yourself when you hurt people you shouldn't, and to use that anger at yourself to motivate change in your behavior. Guilt's purpose is to cause you to do something *better*. To move you toward a better life, better decisions, better relationships, and a closer relationship with God. This kind of positive change begins with recognition of wrong choices and feeling the guilt associated with them. But instead of letting the power of guilt that is God-given force us to change and then forgiving ourselves, we sometimes get stuck in feeling guilt. We absorb guilt into our sense of self and let it place limits on the opportunities of our lives.

Here is a quote from a Calvin and Hobbes cartoon: "There's no problem so awful that you can't add some guilt to it and make it even worse." Think about guilt wreaking havoc in the courtroom of your self-esteem. Ask yourself a question, and be honest. Has someone offered you a chance to serve God, and you thought about doing it until the specter of guilt reminded you of some former misdeed—some failure, some sin—and you pulled back and withdrew yourself from that service? That's the havoc that guilt can bring to our lives.

I wouldn't care so much about the impact of guilt except that it limits the church. Guilt limits the church from reaching maximum effectiveness because there are no "perfect people" in the church. There are no "perfect people" in the world, period. If we're looking for worthiness and perfection as the qualifications for spiritual service, we're going to have to visit heaven to recruit workers because there aren't any perfect people in *this* world. So if the church is going to have any workers, we've got to learn to deal with guilt *effectively*.

Let me share a story with you about a woman I know whose guilt powerfully limited her life. This woman worked at a nonprofit organization just after graduating from college and getting married. She was a bright girl and very likeable and immediately began to have success breathing new life into the struggling nonprofit. Everybody loved her and she loved her job. For a while, life seemed *almost* perfect. Then, through a series of events, she found herself in a situation where she could steal some money from the organization in a manner that would be almost impossible for others to discover. She had never done anything like that before, and she never would have believed she would be tempted to do such a thing; yet, for whatever reason, she took the money.

She rationalized her theft by using the financial limitations she and her family were facing and some harsh treatment she had received from a few of her board members. To her amazement, her action was never discovered. She expected to be caught and waited daily for the humiliation of discovery, but it never came and life went on. It looked like she had managed to pull off the perfect crime, but something irrevocable had been broken within her spirit. She now knew herself to be a thief. In the deepest part of her spirit, she despised herself. She felt like a phony. She began to hate it when people would praise her for her work and flinched emotionally every time someone spoke of her dedication. Week after week she would go to work and wonder if this would be the week that she would be exposed for her duplicity and dishonesty. Her creativity began to suffer and her relationships with her co-workers began to sour. She finally decided that she had to leave her job if she was ever to know any peace.

In spite of stellar job reviews, community praise, and the happiness of her family with their home, she began to make plans to relocate. She knew she could never tell her husband the truth about why she wanted to leave. So she created a cover story about continuing education as the purpose for the change. To her amazement, her husband never questioned her motives and even agreed that it seemed a sensible move for her long-term success. So she quit her job, packed up the family, and moved a thousand miles away to another state. Unfortunately, she learned the hard lesson that distance does not change character, and your self-concept doesn't change just because you have a new address. She made a series of poor decisions which led to her being fired from her new job, and finally she couldn't take the hiding anymore. She approached her pastor in her new town and confessed the whole sordid mess. He counseled her to seek God's forgiveness and to get honest with her husband. She took those painful steps and found that healing began to flow. Her husband forgave her and God renewed her spirit.

She eventually went on to have a successful career and raise a lovely family. When she told me this story, some twenty years had passed since her failure, but she still felt *real* pain when she told me of her weakness. She said,

> I almost destroyed my life, because I couldn't stand my guilt. Do you know how hard it is to go to work and take leadership of an organization, when inside you feel like a fake? Can you imagine how hard it is to hear your family's praise when in your heart you know you are a phony? I let guilt steal years of productivity from my life, and I'll never go there again.

Let me confess that this story is fictional. But it is a compilation of actual experiences from people's lives that I have known. The principles contained in this story are timeless and quite real when you start experiencing the hidden danger of guilt.

- Have you ever done something that you hoped would never be discovered?
- Have you ever been "cursed" by the fact that something you did was not discovered?
- How has guilt caused you to react negatively to the praise of people in your circle of relationships?

The problem with guilt is that it creates limitations to our goals and dreams, which impact relationships and spiritual service. Henry Fielding, the famous English novelist and author of *Tom*

Jones, was reported once to have written that "Guilt has very quick ears to hear an accusation." The Bible says in the book of Proverbs that the sinful man runs when there is no one pursuing (28:1). In other words, it's not hard to intimidate someone with a guilty conscience. When we have a guilty conscience, the devil doesn't have to work too hard to keep us from service because we already feel guilty.

If we feel guilty about something, there are only two options. We can change the action or change our beliefs about the action. That's the concept for dealing with guilt found in pop psychology. Some of that statement I like, but I don't agree with it one hundred percent because it is impossible to change our beliefs about *everything*. If you feel guilty about eating junk food, you've got two choices: you can stop eating Twinkies, or you can decide not to feel guilty about eating those delicious little yellow cakes (which I admit has been my choice many times). But that's a light issue. The place where the pop logic breaks down is that there are certain God-given conscience issues for which you're not going to be able to eliminate the feelings of guilt.

I believe that you can't always just decide not to feel guilty about certain things. Why? Because there are things that, once you do them, God convicts your conscience about. No amount of self-talk will remove these guilty feelings because they are *God-given*. Therefore, we've got to have a better system to deal with that kind of guilt effectively, because when we have a guilty conscience, we become limited in our actions.

I want to be gentle here, and I don't want to hurt anyone. But I also want to be honest. A lot of broken women in our society have been told they don't have to feel guilty about having an abortion. But they're *not able to let go of it.* No matter how much literature these women read, no matter how many times people say what they did was okay, they still feel guilty because they have a God-given conscience that's burdening them. I appreciate an organization that a woman in my community started to provide recovery and healing for women who've been through the trial of abortion. We need to help people recover and love every person burdened by guilt—and many women are struggling with postabortion guilt.

Let me give you an example from the Bible. In the Gospel of John, there is a story in chapter eight that illustrates the limitations of guilt. Jesus had been confronted with a woman who was caught in the act of adultery, and some people wanted to punish her with death by stoning. Jesus' answer to their self-righteousness was, "He who is without sin among you, let him throw a stone at her first" (John 8:7). He means: you are correct in that the Bible does say she should die. But if you're so pure that you can apply this judgment personally, and if you have no sin in your lives, only *then* can you start throwing stones. The Bible says those who heard it "being convicted by their conscience" went out one by one, beginning with the oldest to the youngest until Jesus was left alone with the woman. The consciences of those men kept them from taking action. They could not deny their consciences. And that happens to us in our lives. In this story, examining their consciences benefited the woman, but there are times when our consciences can cause a kind of inaction when we are faced with important decisions. Think about a parent trying to warn a teenager about using drugs, but struggling with the knowledge that they are guilty of doing so in the past. Or consider another parent who has to struggle with the guilt of their own sexual history while trying to counsel their teenager about remaining pure until marriage. These are cases where guilt could slow or hinder someone from doing something they know is right. So what are we to do with our guilt?

First, if possible, we modify our beliefs. In some of the smaller issues of life, we can modify our beliefs because sometimes we have unrealistic attitudes. For instance, we tend to expect perfection in motherhood. Upon reading any of the current parenting literature of our culture, you quickly see that *a lot* is expected of mothers. Unfortunately, mothers are only human. My mother, bless her heart, was a great mom. So when I first started preaching, and I would reference my mother, I would remember all the good things about her, and I would carry on and on about how wonderful my mom was. Once I let her hear a tape of my Mother's Day sermon, and she said, "The women in that church must hate me because, you know, son, I appreciate what you're saying, but I was not *that* perfect." Of course she was right, but we project a model of perfection for women to emulate as mothers. As a result, women sometimes are too hard on themselves and their mothering skills.

Some women have a belief that good moms never lose their tempers with their children. It is implied in our culture that a woman is not a good mom if she ever gets angry at her children. A mom is not even supposed to be irritated or less than kind and loving in any given moment. Maybe you are a mother and you feel guilty because you bought into the exaggeration that good moms don't lose their tempers with their children. You need to examine that belief and even change it by reminding yourself that even the best of moms are only human. Then modify it a little further by adding that if a mom is a follower of Jesus Christ, and if she has truly repented of her loss of temper and no one was hurt by it, then she doesn't need to waste time feeling guilty about it.

Let's consider the origin of guilt as an emotion. As we have already discussed, there are certain guilt feelings that are universal. There is a standard for morality in every culture in the world, no matter the amount of organized religion in that culture. For instance, incest is universally condemned by every culture. Where did that come from? It originates from God. Here's the origin of our guilt. It's inherent, it's genetic, it's in our spiritual DNA. We feel guilt because God implanted in our nature a desire to obey him, and whenever we are disobedient, we feel guilt.

Ever since Eve sinned in the Garden of Eden and Adam followed in her footsteps, people have felt guilty before God. One of their first actions after the original sin was to try and hide from God. Why? Because they felt *guilty* about their disobedience. It is part of our makeup, spiritually, to feel bad when we disobey God. We are wired to feel guilt. Unfortunately, we have magnified the guilt that we are supposed to feel and created something quite different. The guilt God gives us is meant to move us toward a positive change and then be discarded. Yet we have created a pseudo-guilt that we allow to beat us down into psychological misery, even after we have changed our bad behavior. This is utilizing guilt for the wrong purpose. When this happens, we are acting like people who have taken a luxury car and modified it to be a swamp buggy. Luxury cars are not built for driving through mud, brush, and weeds. As humans, we were not built to live in constant mental anguish over failures and faults we have forsaken. People who live that way are using guilt for the wrong purpose.

And not only do we have guilt from our genetic spiritual DNA, but we also have guilt based on our personal choices. Now here's where it gets rough. Most of us can accept that we feel guilty because God wired us for guilt and we are comfortable with that type of guilt. But coming to grips with the guilt that arises out of our personal choices is much more difficult. I suspect that the things we feel most guilty about are not our weaknesses and mistakes in life, but the bad and hurtful behaviors we willingly choose to participate in. Does that sound familiar? The bad and hurtful behaviors we willingly choose seem worse to our consciences. This is the kind of guilt that was eating up Bob, our fictional character at the beginning of the chapter, from the inside out. He knew he had made some poor decisions, and he had no one to blame but himself. So, what is the Christian answer to the hidden danger of guilt? It starts with recognizing that guilt puts a stain on you that limits your life.

A number of years ago, I had an opportunity to preach at a pastors' meeting. I was excited, as this was going to be my first opportunity to speak to a group of pastors. I bought a new shirt and tie especially for the event. The tie was bright yellow and the shirt was white cotton. I felt very confident in my appearance as I went to this fellowship meeting. Unfortunately, a friend of mine came up to me as we were drinking coffee before the service, and he enthusiastically greeted me by vigorously shaking my hand. I had a cup of coffee in my other hand, and the coffee splashed out of the cup and landed on my new shirt and tie. My confidence suddenly disappeared. Instead of looking sharp in a beautiful new tie and a crisp, white shirt, I now looked like I didn't know how to dress for the occasion. And I was going to have to preach with a stain on my shirt. I would have to stand up in front of perhaps the most critical group of people on the planet—fundamentalist Baptist preachers—with a dripping stain on my clothes. I knew from experience that there would be those in the crowd who were going to question everything I did, from which text I used, to which joke I told, to whom I quoted. They were definitely going to talk about my tie. So I tried to hide my coffee stain.

I preached that sermon engaging in some interesting postures. I pulled my coat from side to side in a futile attempt to hide the stain. And how well do you think I preached that sermon? If you are thinking not very well, you are correct. In fact, my speaking ability was quite limited because I was preoccupied with my appearance. The problem was that I had a stain. That stain was probably more visible to me than to anybody else. Now, most of those preachers were nearsighted and probably couldn't see the stain from their seats. But I could see it, and because I could see it, I was intimidated by it, and because I was intimidated by it, it limited my actions and my service. I made the mistake of focusing more on something that had happened to me than on the sermon I was trying to preach. I fear that is exactly what guilt is doing to many people reading this book. They are limiting their service to people and God because they are focusing on something they did instead of on how they can serve, and it's all because of the stain of guilt.

So, what's the answer? We must *get rid* of the stain. When you are talking about a shirt and tie, you can either wash it until the stain comes out, or you can get yourself some new clothes. In the realm of emotional guilt, Christianity gives us even better options. First of all, we must understand that God is interested in our struggle with guilt. And then we need to remember that guilt was dealt with as part of the work of Christ on the cross.

There is a clear teaching found in Romans 3. This passage says plainly that our guilt was dealt with as part of the work of Jesus Christ. Many people know Romans 3:23 by heart because it's a guilt-provoking verse. "For all have sinned and fall short of the glory of God." We read that and say to ourselves, "Yes, that's me, I have sinned!" We read it again and we say, "That verse is true; I surely come short of the glory of God," and we feel pretty bad about ourselves. But have you ever read the verse that follows this painful teaching? "Being justified freely by His grace through the redemption that is in Christ Jesus"

(Rom. 3:24). Do you know what *justified* means? It means to be declared righteous in a court of law. It means that in God's holy court of justice, whenever you've been accused by Satan for your sin of (fill in the blank), God has a plan to deal with your guilt.

For instance, God says, "Kim Beckham, we're going to stand you in front of the bar of justice," and then Satan accuses me of my sins. Immediately, the Lord Jesus Christ stands up as my advocate and says, "I paid for his sin. I redeemed him. I bought him back in my blood," and the Bible says God declares me "not guilty." God then declares that "Kim Beckham is not guilty because he's justified through the redemption found in Christ Jesus." Isn't that wonderful!

The Bibles teaches us in Isaiah 1:18: "Though your sins are like scarlet, they shall be as white as snow; though they are red like crimson, they shall be as wool." He's put our sins behind his back to remember them no more. He's put them in the depths of the sea. He's washed them away in the blood of Jesus Christ. When Jesus Christ looks at you and you've had the life-changing experience of salvation, he sees you in the purity and the blood of Jesus Christ. So why are you feeling guilt? Why are you going around depressed and limiting yourself from serving people when God has already washed all your sins away?

Through the act of confession, believers can maintain their relationship with God. Even committed believers will sometimes find it is their sad experience to sin. In a powerful passage about the struggle of daily Christian life, an apostle who dedicated his life to God, says, "I sometimes do the things I don't want to do, and I sometimes don't do the things I should" (Rom. 7:19, my paraphrase). And if that was true for him, it is certainly going to be our experience as well. The only Christians I know who are sinless are the people who started moving the line of judgment so as not to include the things of which they're guilty.

Do you ever do that? Have you ever tried to lose weight and been struggling to make progress, so you get your scale out and adjust it so it's five pounds off? No doubt a lot of people have indulged in that little personal deception. What are they doing when they do that? They're moving the line so it doesn't include their failure. And that's what people do who claim they never sin as Christians. They just put the thing that troubles them over there on the other side of their mental line of failure and say to themselves, "Oh, that's not a sin." Of course, they are only playing games with themselves, and their consciences will never let them rest with such a cheap parlor trick.

What we need is something stronger and, thankfully, it has been provided. The passage in 1 John 1:9 instructs us, "If we confess our sins, He is faithful and just to forgive us our sins and to cleanse us from all unrighteousness." The good news is that once we face that sin, repent of it, confess it, and turn that sin over to God—and make a genuine attempt to realign our lives with his will—we should no longer beat ourselves up with guilt.

So, let's confess. In some churches they have a phrase, "Tell the truth and shame the devil!" I love the concept of that simple statement. We need to quit hiding and simply admit our spiritual failures. You know one reason people feel so much guilt? It's because they are trying to tell everybody how good they are all the time. Have you ever met people who act like they don't ever do anything wrong when it is obvious to everybody else that they do have faults and failures? We know they are only kidding themselves. So, confess your sins to God. He's faithful and just to forgive your sins and cleanse you from all unrighteousness. That's a powerful step that can lead to immediate freedom from the power of hidden guilt.

Now that you know how to address guilt, here are four practical steps to help you control any new stains of guilt in your life. First, don't do anything wrong! That way you won't ever have any problems with the stain of guilt. Just don't do anything else wrong. Don't do *anything* wrong—ever. None. No more. Nada. Never. Quit. I am being a bit silly here because we all know that's not likely or practical. We've already covered that.

Second, and more realistically, don't continue to do the things that you recognize in your life as being wrong. There may be behaviors that the Holy Spirit has informed you are wrong in your life, and you need to stop them. So simply *stop*. Don't keep it up. Don't do those things any longer! There are certain things that you can't control one hundred percent of the time, but you could make a better effort. Sometimes evil entices us to be lazy in our spiritual lives, and we stop even trying to resist negative behaviors. We give up.

You may be struggling with a sin, and you may have struggled with it a long time. You feel guilty about that behavior. For a while, you manage to do well in that area, even though it's been a struggle. Let me encourage you to *never quit* battling that temptation. Because if you give up to that weakness and just accept it as part of your life, you'll be easily led to a growing disconnect with God. You may find yourself so far away from God you can't find your way back home. Don't *ever* give up the struggle! Refuse to continue to indulge the wrongs you recognize in your life. Get serious about those issues and work to set them right.

Third, as best you can, make amends for the wrongs you have done. You can't always make amends. That's one of the hardest truths of life. You can't always set everything right. I know I wish I could. I wish I could set right some of the wrongs I've done in life, but I can't always do that. In fact, it can be selfish for us to burden people with confessions that they don't need to hear. But, whenever we possibly can, we ought to make things right as far as it's within our power to do so. If there's a situation between you and another person, and you can make it right, make it right. Get right with God and make the best amends you can.

Fourth, learn to manage your guilt effectively. Recognize that there is a difference between honest guilt that leads to confession and change of behavior and pseudo-guilt that wreaks havoc with our self-esteem. How can you tell if you're trapped in pseudo-guilt? If you are still beating yourself up for things that you have admitted to, forsaken, and made all possible amends for, then you should be free of guilt. Any lingering accusations in your mind after taking these steps are the result of an overactive imagination and a hyperstimulated conscience. The key concept in separating false guilt from true guilt is purpose. Ask yourself, "What purpose does this guilt serve?" If its only purpose is to make you miserable, then it's time to abandon it and move on with your life.

Exercises

1. Make a list of the areas of your life in which you tend to hold on to guilt and not let go.
2. After the list is finished, analyze in what area of your life you feel the most guilt. Identify if it is necessary or unnecessary guilt.
3. Keep a guilt journal for a week of any behaviors or relationships in which you carry unnecessary guilt. After one week, burn it or throw it away.
4. If you are struggling with guilt and find these exercises do not help, talk with a professional counselor or clergy at church to identify the root cause of the guilty emotions.

CONCLUSION

Let me tell you a story about a married couple. They thought everything was fantastic in their lives. Their children were healthy, their friendships were many and solid, and their marriage was strong. Things were even going well financially. In fact, since they were doing so well, they decided to do a small remodeling job on one of the rooms in their house.

To their surprise, as they stripped the old wall coverings, they discovered they had termites, and not just a few either—it was a huge infestation. They called the exterminators immediately, but by the time they had cleared out the pests and repaired the structural damage to their home, they had spent nearly twenty thousand dollars!

This unexpected emergency ate up their small savings and the extra money set aside for the remodeling project. The most troubling aspect to them was the realization that the termites had been living in the walls of their home for a long time, silently working to destroy it. They said, "It was a sobering reminder that everything can look good on the surface in your life, but with real damage occurring just out of sight."

Just like those destructive insects, emotional weaknesses can do tremendous damage to many different types of relationships. This book has been written as an attempt to strip away the wall coverings of our emotional lives to expose damaging pests working to harm our connections with those we love. My prayer is that every reader has discovered insights that will help strengthen marriages and friendships. Of course, knowing the pests are there is only the first step. Once we have diagnosed the problem area, we must call in the exterminators to fix the problem and repair any damage that has been done.

Just as with termites, the sooner we recognize the problem, the less damage we will inflict on our bonds of love and friendship by the hidden dangers in our emotional lives. Let me encourage you to bravely strap on your tool belt, pull back the corner of your emotional life, and address these dangers with vigor and persistence. Have the courage and gumption to attack these potential pests. God bless and good hunting.